LIVING IN THE MYSTERY

CRAIG WEIDMAN

Living in the Mystery

Copyright © 2012 by D. Craig Weidman

ISBN 978-0-615-64995-5

Printed in the United States of America

CONTENTS

INTRODUCTION

Imagine having just started to read a really good novel. The plot is just beginning to thicken where you placed your bookmark last night. Today, you are enjoying a latte at your favorite café and overhear the group at the next table talking about the book that's lying on your nightstand. It's right then that it happens. Someone blurts out the ending.

All the anticipation, all the potential adventure—gone, just like that. What's the point in reading the rest of the book now? You know how it turns out. Maybe you will go home and read the next chapter or two tonight. Perhaps over the next few weeks you'll even finish the book. Observing the actions and reactions of the characters will still interest you to some extent, but something will be missing—the mystery of where the plot is leading.

Recently, my son and daughter had urged me to see a particular movie. I had some level of interest in seeing it in the near future, and when they began to tell me the story line, I quickly interrupted them with emphatic urgings to be quiet. They were going to ruin it for me.

There is something about story that intrigues us. A fairy tale, novel, or movie just has to have a little more than "Once upon a time. Yada, yada, yada. And they lived happily ever after." Even *Seinfeld*, the show about nothing, had plot lines that drew viewers in and moved them toward an ending that only made sense from having experienced the story.

Our lives are no different. Often we find ourselves at the outset of some new season of life, and the mystery of what lies ahead makes us want to just jump to the ending. If only someone were at the next table who had already read this book. Sometimes the confusion we face in the middle of one of life's stories causes us to wish there was a fast-forward button so we could just skip past that time of uncertainty.

Looking in upon story as an observer is one thing, but living as the central character in story is quite another. As the outside observer, we are entertained. As a participant experiencing the drama first hand, we are trying to figure out how to navigate the world as we know it at that time. The one looking in upon the story has a vicarious emotional response, and is delighted as the plot takes its turns. The one living inside the story actually experiences the ecstatic highs and gut-wrenching lows all the while trying to make sense of the mystery.

The substance of life is what comes between the beginnings and the endings. There are a lot of things we don't know, a lot of things we can't control in that space between. To live in that space is to live with and in mystery. And that's not a bad thing. In fact, it is inevitable; it is inescapable. When properly embraced, it is beautiful.

Embrace mystery? Sure. Rather than running from it, we lean into it. Rather than trying to avoid it, we move toward it. Rather than rushing to final answers, we ponder new questions. Life is full of mystery. What do we do when we come face to face with it?

There is a man in the Old Testament who is the poster boy for living in the mystery. His is a story of coming face to face with mystery. His story can help us understand our own stories better and what to do with the mysteries that are contained within them. Job is his name, and his story might be one of the most well-known and yet most misunderstood in the entire Bible.

Some view Job's story as an answer to the big question, "Why?" Others see it as a demonstration that "Why?" isn't a question we should ask. I think both perspectives miss the point. The book of Job is often approached with a high focus on the beginning and the ending of Job's story. It is read: "Once upon a time there was a man named Job who lost everything he had—his wealth, his family, and his health. But he stayed faithful to God. (Chapters 1 and 2) Yada, yada, yada. (Chapters 3-41) And he lived happily ever after. (Chapter 42)" From this commonly abridged reading of the book of Job, theological conclusions are made about suffering and the question "Why?"

The part through which we usually skip or glide, the space between the beginning and the ending of the story, is where so much of the real drama is found. It is where we find the unfolding of the story and the very human characters of the narrative. It is here that we find their attempts to deal with and answer tough questions, and ultimately find their struggle to live in the mystery.

The deeper insights and discoveries about ourselves, life, others, God, and simply being in this world will often be found not from the times when things make the most sense, but rather in the places of mystery. In that place of mystery, the world as we thought it to be is turned upside down. Our expectations and assumptions are often proven to be off target. But, in turn, a world of new possibilities is made available.

As you come face to face with the place of mystery, what do you do with it? Some people try to escape it. Others are bent on finding some reasonable explanation for it. Some apathetically exist in it; they fatalistically surrender to it.

The drama of Job leads us to discover something better for how we can understand and respond to the mystery in our lives and in the lives of those around us. There is great wisdom in the story of this most ancient of biblical literature, but it is not the typical fare of conventional wisdom to which we have become so accustomed. It takes us to a place in which mystery can be embraced, leaned into, lived in.

Chapter 1

ONCE UPON A TIME

A television crime drama I religiously watch is aired at 10:00 in the evening, a time by which my wife has usually faded into the la-la land of sleep. Sometimes she will awaken part of the way through the program having missed the beginning. She obviously does not have the benefit of context for where the plot is at the moment and needs to be caught up. Some television programs or movies we watch are such that you can somewhat quickly catch the gist of what's going on within a few minutes of watching. This particular crime drama is not one of them. It falls into a category that, in our family, is called, "You had to see the beginning."

Story is so often that way, whether in fiction or real life. You just need the benefit of the beginning. There is much more to a story than the beginning, but without it you don't have a story. A story's opening gives context to character dialogue, significance to later plot developments and details, and a foundation for what makes this particular story unique. It sets the stage for all that follows and gives some basic meaning to it.

My wife and I often retell to each other the account of our love story up to the particular point in time in which we find ourselves. It may be when we are dreaming together about what may lie ahead in terms of who our children will marry and what it will be like as grandparents. (I can't even believe that word is starting to come onto our radar screen.) Sometimes the reflections come when we've had a day or two in which things have been strained between us, and we try to understand the mystery of how we can love each other so much and yet get so mean with each other. Wondering about what we'll be doing in ten or twenty years will prompt a retelling of the story. Nearly every time, we revisit the beginning of our love story.

"Once upon a time" takes Buffy and me to a place that is over two years before our first date. It was the summer before we entered high school. Buffy attended a week-long Bible school program at our church with one of her friends. Like the stereotypical scene from a romantic comedy movie, I noticed her across the room and for a few moments life moved in slow motion. Somehow, I found out her name during the week, but never once talked to her. I assumed she was out of my league and that I was virtually invisible to her.

It didn't help matters when some of my friends, my brother, and I went to a local community swimming pool toward the end of that week, and there was Buffy with some of her friends. Every part of me wished I were cool enough to just walk up to her and start talking, maybe get to know her. But every part of me at the same time just couldn't break the invisible barrier that made me feel out of her league. (There's that stereotypical romantic comedy thing again.) I would walk past her towel where she sat with Rhonda, Chris, and some guys I didn't know. I would make sure to get in line at the diving board just a few people behind her. That was as close to breaking into her world as I could muster.

Any surges of courage to move in closer were promptly suppressed when I noticed her talking, with apparent ease, to a guy taller, more muscular, and obviously cooler than me. As much as finding your dream girl can be for a fourteen year old, this was it for me. Yet it was so obvious that day at the pool; she would never be mine.

Little did I know until over two years later that she did know who I was and had noticed me like I had noticed her. October 8, 1983 is a day that forever changed my world. I went on my first date with Buffy. Roller skating at the Rollers Roost in Lewistown, Pennsylvania. (Hey, it was the '80s.) The crazy thing is I almost backed out of that date at the last minute. Between the fact that a baseball playoff game I wanted to see was on television that evening (Did I mention I was fairly sheltered and inexperienced at this girls and dating thing?) and that I was scared half out of my wits to now be on the doorstep of doing the thing that had only been a brief dream two years earlier, I called Buffy's friend and said that I was thinking about canceling. In the end, I did go on that date. And as it is said, the rest is history.

That beginning doesn't fully and forever define us and our relationship, but it does help us know from where we have come as we stand in awe at the journey God has allowed us to travel. It is part of being at this place, at this time, in this situation. It teaches us again and again about who we were, who we have become, and that we are still becoming. There may be mystery about what the next step or next chapter is from where we find ourselves right now, but we have some context. The context doesn't answer all the unknowns, but it ties our continuing process of becoming to something and in a small way enables us to live in the mystery.

You are somewhere in a story right now. There is, of course, the grand story of your life in general. But also there is what I like to refer to as "seasons of life." These various seasons are stories in and of themselves. They weave together to create our larger life story. Each has unique characters, plot lines, and outcomes. And each always has a beginning.

Sometimes the beginning is not so clear until after a particular season of life is well under way or is even concluded. Sometimes it is very obvious the moment a new story starts. Either way, there is always a beginning. You might be at the beginning of a season of life right now. You may know it; you may not. Nonetheless, you are at that point with the story yet to unfold in a few predictable ways, but many that are unpredictable. Perhaps you are well into a definite season of life. Looking back you may see where it started, or perhaps where it began is really hard to find. But one thing is sure, there was a beginning.

The beginning, whether recognized immediately or not, gives shape to your story. It sets it into motion. Your choices, responses, and attitudes in the beginning point in the direction of the general trajectory that the plot will follow. Yet also, while giving context and something to which your story ties itself, the beginning is not fully and forever defining of who you are, except to point out that you are still becoming.

None of us has arrived, nor in this lifetime will we ever really arrive. Though sometimes we sure do think we have arrived. That sense of having arrived expresses itself in many ways — spiritually, financially, emotionally, socially, etc. Sometimes we get to places in our lives in which everything just seems right with the world, at least with our own little corner of it. We feel a sense of arrival, maybe not even in a prideful way, but just that life seems so good and all the pieces feel like they are in the right place. Give that some time though, and our world will be undone. There we are reminded that we hadn't arrived; we only had reached a place in which the next stage of our becoming could begin. The Old Testament character Job is a guy who appears to have arrived. (Job 1:1-5) Financially he was well off. He had family and friends. He was regarded by men and God as an upright guy. He was spiritually in tune. The Bible says, "He was the greatest man among all the people of the East." (Job 1:3) And his world was about to be undone. A new stage of becoming was about to begin, and it would be filled with profound mystery.

DYNAMIC SOVEREIGNTY

Job's story doesn't begin like a romantic comedy; it begins more like a crime drama. Let's admit it; we struggle with God's choices in the first two chapters of Job. They don't make sense to us. It sure seems like God aids and abets an assault on Job. Trained theologians and armchair biblical quarterbacks alike have attempted to resolve the tension by painting over this troubling scenario with references to the sovereignty of God. Sometimes it is as if we are told to just trust the sovereignty of God, and we won't be troubled by this passage of Scripture. God's sovereignty, I am afraid, has become a cliché to help us dodge tough, and often times, unanswerable questions instead of it being a mysterious, comforting and unsettling, deeply spiritual reality that is dynamic rather than one-sidedly static.

Sure, we see God's sovereignty all over the first two chapters of Job (and in reality all over the whole book), but let's not just paper over this confounding passage and jump into a simplistic, formulaic prescription for faith. It is not as easy as "trust God's sovereignty and all will eventually work out."

I will never forget when one of the sons in a family we knew from our community died in a fire. As you would expect, it was tragic. Many came to the funeral home the night before the memorial service to give their condolences to the family.

As I waited in line, I thought, "What do I say?"

It was like the inner voice of the Holy Spirit said, "No clichés."

When I arrived before the casket and the grieving family, I first offered a hug to the mother. She immediately, with indescribable grief, sought to make some kind of sense of all this and asked me, "Why would God allow this to happen?"

I only had one answer that made sense in that moment—"I don't know; I wish I did. But you guys are on mine and Buffy's hearts and in our prayers."

Any reference at that moment to God being in control or Him having purposes we don't understand, but can trust, would have sounded presumptive and insensitive. She didn't need theology and Christianese; she needed to know she was not alone in the mystery.

For all of the attempts to explain God's actions in the beginning of Job's story, there is simply much about it all for which we can only say, "I don't know." As Job gets swallowed up in mystery, we look in upon it with some facts that Job didn't have. These facts don't resolve all of the mystery though. They do, however, along with us stepping into Job's shoes, allow us to gain insights into living in the mystery. Hopefully we can do so without being cliché about it.

Though it is mysterious, though it is both settling and unsettling, though it is deeper than we could ever hope to really grasp, God is sovereign. He has a handle on all that's going on now and all that will transpire beyond this moment. Nothing surprises Him or takes Him off guard. Nothing is beyond His scope of understanding or His power to act upon. Yet why do such unspeakable things happen? Why would He allow that which seems so senseless? I don't know. But that's the dynamic reality of His sovereignty; that's where the mystery comes in.

That, too, is where one of the greatest acts of faith comes. Do I lean into Him when I struggle to even find where He is in a situation? Do I surrender my will to His even when I don't really have a clue what His will is about something? Do I trust Him even when everything seems so unpredictable, so undependable at the moment?

Often God's sovereignty is described in terms of God having everything under control. I've often thought of it in this way and have described it as such. It is very much a Christian cliché—"God is in control." But is this really the best way to understand God's sovereignty? In this scenario, we begin to think of God as a grand micromanager pulling all the strings of every person's decisions and every occurrence. We are, then, merely robots programmed to carry out a predetermined sequence of actions within a predetermined, fixed set of conditions.

This denies the very essence of how God made us. Being made in the image of God means having intellect, emotion, and will (or self-determination). Obviously, we possess these in limited fashion and not in perfection as God manifests these qualities of personality. They are further impaired in us by the Fall. But deep in the DNA of every one of us is the ability to choose for ourselves.

Further, the hyper-determinist micromanaging concept of God's sovereignty denies the essence of how God made the world. He set into motion natural laws that make the universe work as it does. Gravity is one of those natural laws. It holds us from floating off into the stratosphere. It also is the explanation for why a sky diver hurdles earthward. So, if I choose to skydive and also choose to be careless in packing my shoot, the result could be a very hard impact with the ground.

Did God make me have a fatal skydiving accident? He knew in advance all the sequence of events and decisions that would lead to the accident. He was not shocked to be looking upon my rapid decent to the earth. But did He pluck me against my will from the safety of my back deck, drag me to the skies, and then hurdle me down toward the ground? Then there is the question of why He didn't just reach out and pluck me from my plunge.

God's sovereignty is more complex than simply saying He controls everything (or that He just put the universe in motion and stands back.) There is a lot about it we don't understand and which is shrouded in mystery, but the opening of Job's story pulls back the veil just a little.

> One day the angels came to present themselves before the Lord, and Satan also came with them. The Lord said to Satan, "Where have you come from?"
> Satan answered the Lord, "From roaming through the earth and going back and forth in it." (Job 1:6-7)

The sovereignty of God causes all of creation to answer to Him. There is universal accountability to God, even by Satan. Satan is shown in these verses coming before God to give account of his activities.

Beyond the realm of this natural world, we often think of God and His good angels over in one corner (a place called heaven) plotting how to bring about good in the world, to defeat the work of Satan, and to help people come to know Jesus. We also have a picture in our minds of Satan and the demons over in another corner (a placed called hell), plotting how to bring about bad in the world, to defeat the work of God, and to keep people from knowing Jesus. Our mental picture of the spiritual world is one in which the two sides never meet and in which Satan is working as hard as possible to be as far as possible away from God.

A conversation between God and Satan is not something we paint into our mind's picture of the spirit world. Yet that is exactly how the Bible paints it in the book of Job. Satan comes along with the angels and presents himself before God. He answers God's questions and asks his own questions of God. The bargaining between God and Satan in Job 1:8-12 and 2:3-6 is fascinating. Much about it is clearly beyond our ability to comprehend, but it does show that there is more to God's sovereignty than simply Him deterministically being in control.

The Little League program through which our son, Paul, grew up, and in which I had coached for four years, utilized teenagers to umpire games at the younger age levels. After Paul had moved on from Little League and was playing at the teenage level, he had the opportunity to umpire some of these games for seven to ten year olds.

It was not uncommon for him to come home after one of those games he umpired and tell us about a coach who argued a call with either him or the other umpire, usually one of his friends. One night in particular he came home to tell us how he had to throw a coach out of the game that night. He told me about how strange it was being a 15 year-old saying "you're outta here" to a grown man in his 30s or 40s. The coach didn't have a choice in the matter at that point; he had to leave the game. On the baseball field, the umpire is in charge.

God's sovereignty, understood as deterministic control, makes Him to be something like the director of a play. He assures that every cast member says what they are supposed to say and when they are supposed to say it. He controls the action, tells the actors where to stand, calls for their entrances and exits, and otherwise directs what is to happen. The people on stage are merely playing roles, acting out a predetermined part.

A dynamic understanding of God's sovereignty, which is reflected not only in the opening scene of Job but also throughout Scripture, means He is more like an umpire. Think about the way in which an umpire is in charge on the baseball field. There are times when a player or coach doesn't have a choice in the matter; what the umpire says goes. It is the umpire's sole discretion and decision to call the game on account of rain. It is the umpire that rules whether a pitch is a ball or a strike or whether a runner is safe or out. That call stands. There are certain rules that govern things like throwing at a hitter or using a foreign substance on the ball. It is the umpire who enforces those rules. Although the umpire is in charge on the field, he doesn't direct the actions of the players. He calls a pitch a strike, but it was the pitcher who decided to throw a fast ball instead of a curve, a slider instead of a change up. The umpire is in charge, but the players have full freedom to play the game as long as they play within the rules.

There are things that are God's call, and His alone. But a vast amount of how our story unfolds hinges upon not only our own decisions but also upon the decisions of others. He gives freedom for those choices to be made and then works with those decisions, which He knew would be made from before the creation of the world, to bring about His purposes in our lives and in this world.

Satan makes an accusation against Job claiming that his faithfulness to God is not authentic.

"Does Job fear God for nothing?" Satan replied. "Have you not put a hedge around him and his household and everything he has? You have blessed the work of his hands, so that his flocks and herds are spread throughout the land. But stretch out your hand and strike everything he has, and he will surely curse you to your face." (Job 1:9-11)

The charge is against not only Job but also, and primarily, against God. In effect, Satan says that Job only serves God because God has controlled the circumstances to assure the outcome of Job's faithfulness. The accusation is intended to demean God—"well of course he serves you; you haven't given him the freedom to reject you, because you are not worthy to be worshipped and served for who you are."

God's response to the challenge of Satan reflects the mysterious dynamic of His sovereignty. "Very well, then, everything he has is in your hands, but on the man himself do not lay a finger." (Job 1:12) God seems to be relinquishing control. Job is placed into Satan's hands to do with him as Satan pleased, within a limitation. This does not diminish God or His sovereignty. It actually serves to glorify Him and magnify His sovereignty.

God's foreknowledge of the choices Satan will make in his attack of Job and of Job's choices in response to his world falling apart means God can release Job into Satan's hands, which will actually turn the tables on Satan and prove him wrong about both Job and God. Job's integrity, though assaulted severely, will prove that indeed he serves God for who He is, not because Job has been bribed into it. Job is indeed a man of authentic faith. And he has been, is, and will continue to be so, because God is worthy of worship simply for who He is.

We see that God gives Satan the freedom to mess with Job's life. But we also see that this freedom is not absolute or un-limited. God may not be the director staging the four calamities that strike Job over the course of verses 13-19, but He does um-pire the situation. There is a limitation to how far Satan can go— he may not bring harm to Job's physical body (at least initially, see Job 2:3-6). God's sovereignty is dynamic but at the same time all things happen within the boundaries of His permission.

Snow globes are a Christmas time favorite for many people. My wife and I have one that is a perennial fixture on our coffee table or an end table. A snow globe usually contains a holiday scene of one form or another—Santa on a rooftop, a decorated tree, shoppers on a sidewalk, etc.—contained in a water-filled ball. Inside the ball with the water and holiday scene are little white particles made to appear as snow. The enjoyment comes when you pick up the snow globe and give it a good shake. The "snow" flies around in a variety of unpredictable directions. The buoyancy of the water gives an effect of snowflakes floating and flittering around in the air. It is mesmerizing and delightful to sit and take in the wonder of the scene.

The path of each individual snowflake is determined by its unique shape. It is also impacted by the paths the other snow-flakes travel as they bump into and/or travel around each other. The movement of the water also influences the motion of the snowflakes. Even the scene through which a snowflake moves tends to impact its direction. The snowflake may settle on Santa's hat or bump off of his nose changing direction.

The movement of all the snowflakes appears rather random and chaotic at first glance. However, there are reasons why any one snowflake travels as it does. Some have to do with the snow-flake itself; others have to do with factors external to the snow-flake. Further, as all of these varied patterns of movement of snowflakes swirl around, they do so within the sphere in which they are contained.

This is a picture of God's dynamic sovereignty and that all things happen within the boundaries of His permission. Our choices, the decisions of others, situations in which we find ourselves, and other factors are given freedom to unfold and create our story line. These are dynamic, variable inputs that substantially impact the trajectory of our lives. Yet it all happens within the sphere of certain boundaries God has established.

We often do not know where those boundaries of God's permission even lie. Job had no clue until the events of verse 13 and following that God had permitted Satan to strike against his wealth and family. And as the calamities began to unfold, Job had no idea how far God would allow it to go.

There is, however, one thing we can know about the sphere of God's permissive will—He will not be moved to act against Himself. In other words, all that He does and allows is in conformity with who He is. He will not do anything that is not in keeping with His infinitely perfect nature or character. The exercise of the free-will of another never compels God to act.

Notice that Satan wanted God to bring calamity upon Job. "But stretch out your hand and strike everything he has, and he will surely curse you to your face." (Job 1:11)

The four calamities that ensued were not the product of God's hand, but rather of Satan's hand within the permission of God. "Very well, then, everything he has is in your hands." (Job 1:12)

Satan sought to ultimately accuse God and baited Him to act against Job not out of perfect love but out of capriciousness. If God responded to Satan's offer, Satan would have had basis to accuse Him of not being good. Though God may act of Himself to bring pain to our lives as part of His loving correction and discipline, He will not capriciously crush us like a curious child would stomp an ant on the sidewalk just because He can.

God's sovereignty is not a predetermined set of whims mechanically imposed upon us, but is a marvelous, purposeful framework reflecting the glory of the person of God within which our lives unfold. That unfolding can be in resistance to Him or in cooperation with Him. Whether or not we really trust Him as we live in the mystery will determine which path we take.

ONE SURE THING

Job's response to the four calamities that fell upon him mysteriously and without any apparent warning is confounding. "At this, Job got up and tore his robe and shaved his head. Then he fell to the ground in worship." (Job 1:20)

If not after the second or third calamity, certainly after the fourth, most of us would begin thinking, "God, you had better have a pretty good explanation for this." We would try to make sense of the mystery.

But what do we do when we just can't make sense of the mystery? Job went to the only place that made any sense. He did the only thing that he knew he could do in the middle of the incomprehensible. He went to God, and he worshipped. Why God? Why worship? Because Job trusted God. He had grown to know that no matter what happened he could entrust himself into the hands of God. The very place Satan hoped to make unsafe for Job was the place where Job felt the safest. God was his one sure thing in the mystery of his suffering.

One Friday night when I was ten years old, I came into the house sweaty and tired from playing. It was one of those hot, humid summer evenings. Badly needing a drink, I poured some lemonade and proceeded to gulp down the whole cup of it without taking a breath. Almost immediately I began to have a bit of a stomach ache. The mildly blah feeling that I had, at first thought was simply from drinking too fast, gradually became a sick feeling. It came time for bed, but I struggled to sleep. I felt that at any moment I would throw up. It appeared that I had come down with a case of stomach flu.

The pain in my stomach began to change throughout the night. By one or two in the morning, not only did I have nausea but I was also beginning to have piercing pain concentrated in my lower right abdomen. The pain became so acute within another hour or so that I was curled up in a ball on our living room floor with my parents trying to comfort me. A bout of projectile vomiting seemed to temporarily ease the pain, but my mother was concerned. Remembering her own symptoms with appendicitis when she was a teenager prompted her to suggest that I be taken to the emergency room. At 3:30 AM my mom drove me to the local hospital three miles from our home while my dad stayed behind with the other kids who were still sleeping.

The next three hours was some pretty unsettling stuff for a ten year old. An emergency room isn't the most kid friendly place to begin with, but then there was blood taken, an IV line inserted into my arm because I had become dehydrated, doctors and nurses I didn't know poking and prodding me, and a trip on a gurney through what seemed to be dungeon corridors to have X-rays taken. By 7:00 AM there was a diagnosis of acute appendicitis, and I was being rolled in for emergency surgery.

Anesthetic was added to my IV. Ten, nine, eight, sev... My eyes slowly opened, and for a moment I wondered where I was. There was a television mounted on the wall. I heard my mom's voice. I looked and there sitting by my side in the hospital room were both of my parents. It was Saturday afternoon.

From beginning to end throughout the uncertainties of that brief ordeal was one sure thing for me—my parents. They were the familiar in the middle of things that didn't make sense to me. I didn't know what was happening to me, but I did know my parents, who were there with me through it. And that made all the difference in the world.

Out of depth of relationship with God comes the strong trust that carries us through crisis. He is our one sure thing in the mystery because we know Him and He is there with us through it.

STRUGGLE

Knowing God and trusting Him doesn't take the mystery out of life though. It actually enables us to embrace deeper mystery. It doesn't answer all the questions, nor does it resolve all the uncertainties. Leaning into the reality of God being our one sure thing in the mystery of suffering doesn't magically remove the struggle.

Have you ever had one of those days that started out bad and only went downhill from there? Sometimes a whole week can end up going this way. By the time you get to Friday, the prior Monday is looking pretty good.

It's one thing to have a bad day or week, but there are those seasons in our lives that are something more than just a bad day or a bad week. A few major stressful events over the course of several months or a year can be enough to completely overwhelm us. One crisis seems to come after the other like one wave crashing in on top of the next along a storm driven beach.

You surrender yourself into God's hands as Job did: "The Lord gave and the Lord has taken away; may the name of the

Lord be praised." (Job 1:21) Then the next wave rolls over you. Just when you think you can't take anymore, you get hit with more. That's the nature of a season of struggle, and strong trust in God does not make us immune to it.

It wasn't enough that Job lost all of his wealth and his children; he then is struck with unbearable physical suffering.

> So Satan went out from the presence of the Lord and afflicted Job with painful sores from the soles of his feet to the top of his head. Then Job took a piece of broken pottery and scraped himself with it as he sat among the ashes. (Job 2:7-8)

Satan is persistent, and often times we underestimate his commitment to our destruction. Remember what Jesus said: "The thief comes only to steal and kill and destroy." (John 10:10) Satan wasn't about to give up on Job easily.

Satan had thrown a flurry of four punches, but they didn't land where he had hoped they would. Job was suffering, but instead of cursing God like Satan had predicted, he was leaning into God. Like a boxer pursuing his opponent, Satan kept up the pressure.

A boxer on the attack doesn't throw a few punches and then retreat to his corner to see what happens. He doesn't let up; he keeps on the pressure; he follows a series of jabs with a left hook and a right uppercut. The jabs aren't enough to take down the opponent; they simply soften him up and make him vulnerable to the follow-up punches.

Satan's left hook was a physical attack on Job's body. Initially God had drawn the line there. Satan could not come after Job's health unless the boundaries of God's permission allowed it. Now Job's health was within those boundaries, and Satan took full advantage.

He didn't just throw the left hook; he immediately delivered a right uppercut as well. "His wife said to him, 'Are you still holding on to your integrity? Curse God and die!'" (Job 2:9) This isn't just anyone suggesting that Job curse God; it was his own wife, the one closest to him. Satan went for the knockout. He wouldn't settle until he had done all he could to move Job to curse God.

Satan will come at you and me with every dirty trick he can. He will use up the full limits of the boundaries that God's permission allows. To underestimate his resolve to derail us in our journey is to be unprepared for one of the aspects of the struggle that comes with living in the mystery.

PERSPECTIVE

A swimmer pushed under the surf by successive ocean waves can quickly become disoriented. The rush of uncertainty piles up. Where is the shoreline? Which direction am I facing? How deep is the water? If the swimmer surrenders to panic, the situation only worsens.

What do we do when the rush of life's uncertainties piles up? One response, like the panicked swimmer, is to surrender to anxiety. Another is to seek perspective. Perspective is not having all the answers, solutions, or outcomes for life's challenges, concerns, and other mysteries: When will I find a job? Who, if anyone, will I marry? Will my investments recover in time to afford my children's college education? What are the details of this call I have from God? Why am I having all these physical problems? Is the waywardness of my child my fault? For these and a thousand other questions, perspective keeps us from becoming disoriented as the waves come in upon us.

There are two key truths that if we embrace will carry us a long way toward maintaining perspective in the places of mystery. The first is that bad things happen to good and bad people alike. The simple fact of being alive in this world, of getting out of bed in the morning and going about our day, means we will encounter the stuff of life. Sometimes we'll bang our foot on the bedpost while we are still trying to focus our eyes first thing in the morning. It has nothing to do with our righteousness or lack thereof. It is simply because the bedpost was there, we have a foot, and we were not quite fully awake yet.

For some reason, many Christians expect God to provide them a sheltered existence here on this earth, especially when they are being particularly faithful to Him. Job's wife was like this. Her life philosophy, which is shared by far too many Christians in western churches, would actually wish that Satan's charge against God were true—that indeed God did put a hedge around believers to keep the troublesome stuff of life from making them uncomfortable. If you think it is not true, consider one of the prayers most of us have prayed; "Lord, make the sun shine for our church picnic." But should God give sunshine for the church picnic any more than He should give rain to the agnostic farmer whose land is next to the church?

Jesus said:

"But I tell you: Love your enemies and pray for those who persecute you, that you may be sons of your Father in heaven. He causes his sun to rise on the evil and the good, and sends rain on the righteous and the unrighteous." (Matthew 5:44-45)

Sometimes a rainy day is a nuisance; sometimes it is a benefit. Righteous and unrighteous alike should expect to sometimes have outdoor plans ruined by a rainy day. That's just the way life is. A flu bug takes up residence in our body; our car is totaled because of driver error on ours or someone else's part; a burglar breaks into our home. That's just the way life is. These are the experiences of living in the real world.

Job was living in the real world even as he struggled to live in the mystery. "Shall we accept good from God, and not trouble?" (Job 2:10) He was as ready to accept calamity as part of life as he was an increased fortune. The perspective formed by his understanding and embracing of this truth would help sustain him in this deepest of valleys in which he found himself.

Yes, followers of Christ will enjoy the painless, annoyance-free experience of the new heaven and new earth one day, but until then we experience this earth. And sometimes that experience is more hell on earth than heaven on earth. To come out of the fantasy that we should be sheltered from the annoying, frustrating, painful stuff of life leads to perspective.

The other perspective developing truth is that our trials are God's material for strengthening us and glorifying Himself. "In this you greatly rejoice, though now for a little while you may have had to suffer grief in all kinds of trials. These have come so that your faith—of greater worth than gold, which perishes even though refined by fire—may be proved genuine and may result in praise, glory and honor when Jesus Christ is revealed." (1 Peter 1:6-7) The four calamities that formed the first test of Job deepened the authenticity of his faith in God and prepared him for the dark night that was soon to come upon him.

Then the Lord said to Satan, "Have you considered my servant Job? There is no one on earth like him; he is blameless and upright, a man who fears God and shuns evil. And he still maintains his integrity, though you incited me against him to ruin him without any reason." (Job 2:3)

It also proved Satan wrong and God to be worthy of worship for who He is.

We admire Job's perseverance and recognize "what the Lord finally brought about." (James 5:11) We are inspired by familiar passages on the value of trials and testing.

> ...we also rejoice in our sufferings, because we know that suffering produces perseverance; perseverance, character; and character, hope. And hope does not disappoint us, because God has poured out his love into our hearts by the Holy Spirit, who he has given us. (Romans 5:3-5)

> Consider it pure joy, my brothers, whenever you face trials of many kinds, because you know that the testing of your faith develops perseverance. Perseverance must finish its work so that you may be mature and complete, not lacking in anything. (James 1:2-4)

But do we live in this reality? Do we enter into the mystery with a sense of anticipation for how we will be formed and shaped and with wonder and awe over the chance to bring glory to God in our lives through endurance of the test?

Job did not enjoy the valley through which he traveled, but he also did not reject the mysterious gift that the dark season presented him. Our greatest times of development and formation rarely come from the places of great ecstasy but from the places of great pain. Often we resist when a season of darkness begins to unfold, but it is a time when real and deep treasure can be found.

INTEGRITY

The trait that we are prone to most attribute to Job is perseverance. Indeed, he persevered. His perseverance is noted in the New Testament in James 5:11. But his perseverance was an outcome of a deeper quality. Job was first and foremost a man of integrity. It was this quality that God particularly noted to Satan at the end of the first test. God did not say to Satan, "Do you see his toughness" or "Your attacks were no match for his grit and tenacity." No. God said, "Job has integrity." Can that be said of me? Can it be said of you?

There are a variety of ways to define integrity. It is being the same in private as in public. It is doing the right thing even when no one is looking. Integrity suggests consistency of character that is upstanding and right. Integrity is an expression of godly character that is maintained no matter what.

Integrity is an invaluable asset, not because it is a means to some end but simply for itself. Integrity is an ethical and moral anchor that keeps us from drifting this way and that with the current of changing circumstances.

The beauty and power of integrity is that when all else is lost, nothing can take away this most valuable asset. Integrity is crucial to living in the mystery. Our job can be taken away by downsizing, organizational realignments, or outsourcing. Our house may be taken from us by fire or governmental eminent domain. Our car can be taken by theft or accident. Someone we love can be taken from us by death, relational conflict, or a long distance move. Integrity, however, cannot be taken away; it can only be given away.

God has given us what we need to hold on to our character, to hold on to our integrity. "His divine power has given us everything we need for life and godliness through our knowledge of him who called us by his own glory and goodness." (2 Peter 1:3) As we live in the mystery, we lean into God for integrity that will guide us through the uncertain circumstances of the dark night.

Chapter 2

WHY?

It was a thrill for my wife and me to hear our children's first words. That first "da, da" or "mum, mum" is the beginning of language development. We would try to coax Paul and Adrean to mimic our sounding out of those simple words. Of course there was the friendly contest between Buffy and me to see which of us would win the prize to have our name uttered first.

I remember thinking about what it would be like to hear my children someday speak in full sentences. I was so anxious for the time to come when we wouldn't have to guess what that little one was thinking by interpreting their pointing and "goo goo ga ga" sounds. Thoughts expressed in coherent language would make it so much easier.

And it did get easier, but only for a little while. The cognition of a two or three year old is relatively simple; therefore, communication is fairly straightforward. If he is hungry, he says, "I'm hungry" or "I want Cheerios." She tells you during potty training, sometimes ninety seconds too late, "I have to go to the potty." They express their need; we meet the need; life is good.

That is except when they throw a tantrum because we said, "No." Hence the term, "terrible twos."

Then something happens in those preschool years. Simple statements of request (or demand) begin to be supplemented with questions. By the time kindergarten rolls around, you are receiving a steady diet of sentences which begin with that small, and yet huge, word WHY. Why do we have two ears? Why do we have one nose? Why is there hair in grandpa's ears and nose? Why does thunder make a big noise? Why is there lightning? Why does it rain? You get the picture.

One day our family was driving in the car and one of our kids, about five or six years old at the time, started to chase down what seemed to be every mystery that could exist in the mind of a child that age. My little child's curiosity had more stamina than my ability to keep up. Eventually I had to ask, "Can you please give daddy a rest?"

The next words that came from the back seat were "Why do you need a rest daddy?"

Fortunately, God's stamina is more than enough for all of our childlike questions. And He receives those questions with delight, because so many of our questions reflect curiosity and a desire for discovery. The development of young children is aided through their questions. Without those questions, learning and growth in understanding would come very slowly, or not at all. We do a disservice to others in the body of Christ, especially to those young in their faith journey, when we discourage them from asking "Why" of us or of God. This is one of the key ways in which they develop spiritually.

Ten years after our children were in kindergarten and that wearying drive during which I needed a rest from questions about ear and nose hair and the causes of weather events, sentences starting with the word "Why" were still coming my way. Only now they had a different tone and purpose. Why can't I go out with my friends tonight? Why do I have to pay for putting gas in the car? Why can't I just skip school today? Why does it matter to you if my room is a mess? Why won't you buy me those concert tickets?

Innocent curiosity and discovery are not at the heart of these questions. They are a test of the boundaries and an attempt to secure more freedom than has been granted. They are not an inquiry to learn or gain understanding but a challenge to get one's own way. When laced with a spirit of rebellion these questions are unproductive and detrimental to maturation; otherwise though, this type of questioning serves a developmental, formative purpose. If a teenager lives passively, only unquestionably doing everything she is told to do, letting others completely define her, and never forging her own volitional identity, she will not be prepared for adulthood. She will be dependent, helpless, and subject to be carried along by the whim of anyone.

Similarly, maturing Christians will have questions that are not so much born of innocence inquiry. Discovery is not really the crux of their sentence that begins with "Why." It is a test of the boundaries. It is an attempt to find out just where God stands and what freedom we can exercise. I'm not talking about rebellion, but the give and take of a growing relationship. It is one thing for God to have a clear line on something and for us to decide that there is no good reason for it as far as we're concerned, so we are intent to cross that line in the final analysis. That is rebellion and a place we are not permitted to go. But it is a far different thing for us to wrestle with the purpose behind something God has revealed or called us to do as we try to find reasons to help us submit to His will. This is part of growing up in faith.

My children are now adults, and they still have questions for my wife and me. The same has been true for me too. I didn't stop asking my parents "Why" when I became an adult. Shortly after I began in ministry as a pastor, I called my parents one Sunday afternoon. I felt so fatigued and was rather discouraged with the way the ministry was going at my first church. My question that day was, "Why is ministry so hard?"

Mom and Dad were able to share some insights and wisdom. It was good to find out that it is not abnormal for a pastor to feel drained after a full Sunday morning of ministry and preaching. They also gave good counsel that I not make any major decisions on a Sunday evening or Monday, to wait a few days to gain some perspective after I've recouped from the drain of Sunday.

There is a third kind of question that Christians have for God. These are the questions of the mature, of those who have done much growing up but know they still have growing to do. These are questions for gaining insight and deeper understanding of God and His ways. They are the questions most likely not to have easy or ready answers. Often they remain only partially answered or even unanswered, not because God doesn't love or care about us but because the outstanding question produces more growth than the answer would.

All three types of questions—childlike curiosity, testing the boundaries, and gaining insight—are part of spiritual growth and development. They are part of a growing relationship with God. They are not improper as so many have come to believe and teach. Questions, when asked with the right attitude, are essential to any relationship, and our relationship with God is no different. Perhaps nothing prompts questions for our Heavenly Father more than when things happen that don't make sense or when we are in a season of life filled with uncertainties. "Why" is a vital part of living in the mystery.

Consider all the whys Job had in chapter 3:

- *"Why* did I not perish at birth and die as I came from the womb?"
- *"Why* were there knees to receive me and breasts that I might be nursed?"
- *"Why* was I not hidden in the ground like a stillborn child, like an infant who never saw the light of day?"
- *"Why* is light given to those in misery, and life to the bitter of soul?"
- *"Why* is life given to a man whose way is hidden, whom God has hedged in?"

This is some pretty intense stuff. We feel the depth of his confusion, the seeming senselessness of it all. What would we say to him as his friend? How would we deal with it if we were in his shoes?

THE BEAUTY OF SILENCE

Before I entered pastoral ministry, I worked with my parents operating the Christian radio station they owned from the mid-1980s to the early 1990s. One late morning, about an hour or so before lunchtime, a call came to the station from the police informing us of "an incident involving a train" that had closed a local road so we could announce traffic was being instructed by police to stay away from the area.

The on-air announcement was being prepared as we decided who would go to where the incident had occurred in case there was something newsworthy to report. It was determined that I would go to the scene. I jumped into my car to make the ten mile trip.

The short journey took me along a main highway to an exit for the small town near the area where the incident was reported to have happened. The highway on which I was traveling ran along the side of a small ridge and overlooked a valley. The road that was closed by police ran along the other side of the valley. As I approached the exit, I looked to my right across the valley and saw smoke rising in the general area of where police had reported the incident.

My mind began to race about what I might encounter in a few minutes. I got off at the exit and drove through Thompsontown. Not far out of town, but before arriving where the smoke rose into the air, I came upon a police barricade. Just getting out of another car was a reporter for another radio station in the area. The two of us proceeded to walk together the mile or so from there to the source of the rising smoke where the road disappeared beneath a two or three-story high pile of coal and train wreckage.

Two trains had collided. One had run a switch stop and both ended up on the same track traveling directing at each other. Neither train could stop in time to prevent the tragedy that took the lives of all the crew members on both engines. When I first arrived, I was stunned speechless by the magnitude of what I saw. And the words which eventually did come and have been used in the years since to try to describe that scene really can't capture what I saw and experienced that day.

Life's toughest trials can come at us like a train on the wrong track. The collision wrecks our world and leaves us and those around us without words to fully describe it. It is made all the more indescribable when the challenge or difficulty seemingly has no good reason, no clear cause and effect. "Why" becomes a gut wrenching cry for some kind of explanation.

As wonderful as an explanation would be, there is also the beauty of silence. While we wait for heaven to provide a reason or purpose, there is wisdom in us not trying to figure out ours or someone else's mystery. Sometimes the inexplicable needs to remain unexplained.

Three of Job's friends came to see him, and what they encountered was an unexpected, unimaginably wrecked human being.

When Job's three friends, Eliphaz the Temanite, Bildad the Shuhite and Zophar the Naamathite, heard about all the troubles that had come upon him, they set out from their homes and met together by agreement to go and sympathize with him and comfort him. When they saw him from a distance, they could hardly recognize him; they began to weep aloud, and they tore their robes and sprinkled dust on their heads. Then they sat on the ground with him for seven days and seven nights. No one said a word to him, because they saw how great his suffering was. (Job 2:11-13)

These guys were stunned into silence. Having completed the customary ritual (Tearing their clothes and putting dust on their heads was an outward, visual symbol of grief.) to identify with Job in his suffering, they just sat there by his side without a word for seven days. The intensity of the situation Job faced was so great he didn't even look like himself. What do you say to that?

Yet don't we, when faced with those kinds of word-robbing encounters with someone's deep struggle, begin trying to think of something deep or profound to say? We try to come up with words that can either explain or just make it all feel better. The reality is, though, that there are times when words just won't do. To try to come up with some may only make matters worse for the one we are trying to comfort, whether it is trying to comfort ourselves or another.

The three friends began on the right track when they didn't say anything. They may have been so shocked and utterly overcome that they were simply left speechless for so long, or they may have had some initial wisdom which prompted them to just sit with Job. Either way, there was beauty in the silence. It said, "Job, we're here; we don't understand, but we're here." Presence would speak louder than any words could have.

Eventually they succumbed to what is our natural tendency— to say something, anything, that might help bring some sense to a senseless situation. Beginning in Job 4 and continuing for the next twenty-one chapters, the three friends drone on and on as they attempt to deal with why Job must be suffering so much. Rather than live in the mystery, they had to devise some rational explanation.

Rather than help Job, they made his suffering worse, because explanations don't heal brokenness. At the end of the explanation, you are still broken. You still hurt. You still need recovery and healing.

Think about the last time you dropped a dish and it shattered to pieces. If you are like me, you spent the next minute or two talking to yourself out loud. "How did I do that? What is wrong with me? I'm sure I was holding onto it well. What happened?"

One time my wife said to me, "Standing there talking about it isn't going to make it be unbroken." She was right. Even if I could definitively determine how the dish got from my hand to the floor, the dish is still broken.

There certainly is a place for reflection, but could it be that we analyze, hypothesize, and surmise as we do, hoping that if we get it all figured out the brokenness will go away, or at least not feel so bad? Through our explanations we try to heal ourselves

and others. Instead of trusting that "the
brokenhearted" (Psalm 34:18) and that
hearted and binds up their wounds" (F
explain the situation that is inexpli
perspective.

Wisdom would lead us to leave some ⌐
unexplained. It is often in the beauty of silence that we meet the
Healer, not so much even for the healing but simply for Himself.

DESPERATION DISTORTS PERSPECTIVE

The story is told about a couple of men who worked alongside of
the inventor Thomas Edison. At one point in their work, they
became frustrated by their lack of progress. One failed experi-
ment after another had discouraged them. Finally one of them
said, "What a waste! We have tried no less than seven hundred
experiments and nothing has worked. We are not a bit better off
than when we started."

Edison, the persistent, patient, undeterred man that he was,
replied, "Oh yes we are! We now know seven hundred things
that won't work. We're closer than we've ever been before."

Life can leave us feeling like Edison's frustrated assistants.
We try and try, but it seems all we are doing is spinning our
wheels. Setback upon setback can quickly discourage us. Then at
some point we are pushed beyond mere discouragement.
Discouragement is bad enough, but there is a place we can reach
when the struggle begins to feel too much and we slip into
despairing of our situation.

Desperation is like hard rain on the windshield. The wipers
seem to barely keep up. We try to press on in the storm, but it is
difficult to see. The view before us is blurred and fuzzy through

ent. We have a destination to reach, but continuing on is
st impossible when there is an intense downpour. There are
mes when pulling to the side of the road, gathering our bearings, and proceeding when the worst of the storm passes is the
best course of action.

Desperation distorts our perspective. It makes our outlook on
life fuzzy. It blurs our view of God, His purposes, ourselves, and
others around us. Pressing on in the storm that swirls in our soul
appears impossible due to the intensity of what we are experi-
enceing. Conventional wisdom says the strong are those who
learn to tough it out and power through. True wisdom, though,
teaches us that it is not about how strong we are, but rather how
strong the One is in whom our faith rests. The best course of
action may be to pull over and just wait for the Lord to move the
storm on.

Reaching our breaking point isn't necessarily a bad thing,
because it can lead us to understand how frail we really are and
how wonderful the working of God's power in our frailty really
is. As the apostle Paul put it:

> But we have this treasure in jars of clay to show that this
> all-surpassing power is from God and not from us. We are
> hard pressed on every side, but not crushed; perplexed, but
> not in despair; persecuted, but not abandoned; struck down,
> but not destroyed. (2 Corinthians 4:7-9)

The intensity of Job's suffering pushed him across the line
between discouragement and desperation. The jar of clay was
much more real to him in chapter 3 than the all-surpassing
power of God that would eventually radiate through the cracks
of his life. As a result, his perspective began to be lost.

None of us can really blame Job for reaching the place in which he wished he had never been born. (Job 3:1) Any of us would have likely felt the same way. Indeed, many of us likely would have gone even farther had we been subject to the depths of the inexplicable as he was. Would you or I have gone so far to validate Satan's claim by cursing God?

Though he crossed the line from discouragement into desperation and though his perspective blurred, he did not cross the line and curse God, the thing Satan wanted for Job even more than misery. He did not curse God, but he did question why God would have allowed him to even be born to experience this. His perspective was distorted. He had forgotten the many joys of life which he had the opportunity to have experienced because he was born. He was unable to see anything but pain and suffering.

Being swept up in a dark, painful moment can make us lose sight of realities beyond that moment. Something happens in the middle of the soul like what happens in the dead of winter in middle to late January in the northeastern United States.

My wife and I have lived our whole lives (except me for a few years when I was a very little child) in a region of the United States (the northeast) that experiences all four seasons of the year. My favorite is autumn—crisp air, changing leaves, football, smells of harvest. Spring and summer are my wife's favorites. For her it comes down to the feel of the warm sun. I like spring and summer too, and Buffy appreciates autumn. But we both have some pretty mixed feelings about winter.

A few snow flurries filling the air in early December makes things feel festive as the Christmas season gets under way. Light snow giving us an inch or two Christmas Eve is so nostalgically Currier and Ives. We don't even mind one big snow storm the first week or so of January. But by the end of January, especially one that has been cold and icy, we are just tired of winter.

A couple weeks of pure winter with bitter cold, snow, clouds, and more hours of darkness than sunlight seem to erase the joy of the past summer at the beach and cooking out. It makes us almost forget the beauty of spring flowers and autumn leaves. It's only a few weeks removed from the festivities of Thanksgiving and Christmas, but feels like a lifetime apart. It is no accident that people experience more depression in the middle of winter. In the dead of winter, everything is just so stark, and it seems like this is our only reality.

A winter in the soul can be quite stark. It can leave us feeling spiritually, emotionally, and mentally cold. It can envelop us in despair and distort our perspective.

FIXATION

Momentary lapses of perspective are understandable and sometimes to be expected when the darker experiences of life are upon us. But it is a dangerous place to stay for very long. Anxious brooding draws us into more anxious brooding like a downward pull on our souls.

We see Job getting sucked more deeply into despair as he flails about trying to get a grasp on "why." First, he cursed the day of his birth. (Job 3:1-16) The next natural step was for him to wish he were dead. (Job 3:20-22). But death wasn't coming to release him from the struggle, and the only thing left in his focus was misery. He could no longer see anything good, only the bad.

> For sighing comes to me instead of food; my groans pour
> out like water. What I feared has come upon me; what I

dreaded has happened to me. I have no peace, no quietness; I
have no rest, but only turmoil." (Job 3:24-26)

The more he fought against the mystery that had surrounded
him, the more he despaired of having no sensible answers. Fixation can trap us in the place of despair. It is like the soul is being
swallowed in quicksand.

Quicksand was a staple of old, cheesy movies. As a result of
the exaggerations depicted on screen and our ignorance about
the mysterious soup, most of us would have to admit being
afraid of the stuff. We picture stepping off the edge of solid
ground into a pit containing a sandy blob that gradually swal-
lows us alive if someone doesn't come along to throw us a rope
and pull us to safety.

The reality is that if you step into quicksand, it won't suck
you down of its own accord. Further, it would be rare to step
into quicksand that is deep enough to be over your head that
you would in effect be swallowed up by it. However, the nature
of your movements can cause you to dig yourself deeper into it
and be trapped.[1]

Scientists explain that the key is to not panic and to allow
yourself to float to the surface. Floating in quicksand doesn't initially sound like a possibility, but quicksand is denser than water
and means you can more easily float in quicksand than in water.
"The worst thing to do is to thrash around in the sand and move
your arms and legs through the mixture. You will only succeed
in forcing yourself down into the liquid sandpit. The best thing
to do is make slow movements and bring yourself to the surface,
then just lie back. You'll float to a safe level."[2]

Questions are part of a healthy process for growth and development and need to be part of living in the mystery. There come
times, though, when the questions with which we wrestle have

no ready answers and begin to form into panicked, thrashing movements that force us downward into despair. Anxiety takes over and becomes a vicious cycle that robs us of the treasure that can be discovered in the dark times. This isn't fatalistic resignation; rather it is recognition that there is more to the story than just what we can now see and feel.

When we feel the grip of fixation and downward cycle of anxiety upon our soul, it is a time to intentionally release that which confounds, challenges, or otherwise overwhelms us. This is what the apostle Paul meant when he wrote, "The Lord is near. Do not be anxious about anything, but in everything, by prayer and petition, with thanksgiving, present your requests to God. And the peace of God, which transcends all understanding, will guard your hearts and your minds in Christ Jesus." (Philippians 4:5-7) Instead of fighting against the mystery, we lie back into the transcendent peace of God that will hold us at a safe level.

REFOCUS

The first time I took each of our children out on the roads when they were learning to drive was an experience filled with a rush of emotions. There was the obvious one of fear, but there was also excitement and pride as a new adventure began in their lives. It also brought a sense of nostalgia as I reflected upon how quickly this child of mine had grown up. But amid all that was going on inside of me, I had to find a place of calm, at least outwardly, to be a voice of reassurance, encouragement, and steady guidance as we ventured into traffic.

They both could hardly wait to get out there. Then when the time came to actually pull out of our driveway and into a real live driving situation, they suddenly weren't so confident. Quickly they were making a mistake that is common to most new drivers—zeroing their eyes in on the road and situation right in front of the car.

Of course a driver needs to be alert to things immediately ahead, but the eyes need to do more than just look at the front edge of the engine hood and 100 feet of pavement beyond that. It is important to scan to the left and right as well as farther down the road. This provides a larger context and perspective within which to smoothly and safely navigate the vehicle.

The way I helped Paul and Adrean gain confidence and ability in their driving was to gradually increase the intensity of the situation each time I would take them out. Initially, we would trek through surrounding neighborhoods on streets with slower speed limits and fewer cars. The next time out we would venture onto some of the main streets in our community that had more traffic at just a little higher speeds. Eventually, I would work them up to the point at which I would direct them onto Interstate 95, which ran nearby our home.

The day Adrean had her first adventure onto I-95 is one I'll not likely ever forget. She had been progressing fairly well and gaining more confidence. It was time to take that last big step. We were headed down Business Route 1 past the Oxford Valley Mall and the series of car dealerships that lined what was locally known as Lincoln Highway.

At the red light just before reaching the interchange for I-95, Adrean asked, "Are we headed down to Penndel?"

I said, "No, follow that sign for 95 North toward Trenton."

"I don't know if I'm ready," she replied with a sense of growing fear in her voice.

I told her that she would do just fine and to go ahead and take the ramp onto 95. The light turned green, she drove through the intersection and put on her right turn signal to move onto the entrance ramp. She accelerated up the ramp, and as she approached moderately heavy traffic moving at a high rate of speed on the interstate, I could see the panic taking over her body.

Her hands squeezed down hard on the steering wheel; she began to breathe more rapidly; and her eyes fixated to that zone of blacktop just ahead of her while pleading with me, "I can't do it; I can't do it."

Adrean eventually got her bearings, but the intensity of the situation and the speed at which things were happening during those initial anxious moments caused her focus to be too limited. She needed to refocus her eyes on the bigger picture. She needed to shift from looking only at 100 feet of pavement just beyond the front of the car to looking for the traffic that may have been slowing a quarter mile down the road, for the signs that gave direction, and for other conditions that would inform her journey.

Refocus is the antidote for fixation. When we zero in only on the things that don't make sense, we simply can't see the things that do make sense and miss out on the guidance it provides. We need to refocus when things just don't make sense by shifting from the "why" of our existence to the "who" of our existence.

There is nothing wrong with asking "why," but if we are not careful, a form of "why me" can surface that puts self at the center. This has the effect of dethroning God in our lives and disconnects us from the one thing that provides sense and guidance in the mystery. When we get to this place, refocus is needed to prevent us from descending into self-absorbed disconnection from God.

Job's eyes got zoned in on the pavement immediately in front of him. His hands were anxiously gripped on the steering wheel of his life as he cried out, "I can't do this; I can't do this."

He didn't know why God had him on this road, but the Heavenly Father understood what Job didn't yet understand— that this road would bring about further growth and development in his life. He struggled to refocus because of the narrow theologies of his three friends, as we'll see in later chapters. But eventually another friend and a powerful encounter with God refocused Job and kept him from being totally defeated.

What is the hundred feet of pavement in front of you upon which your gaze is anxiously fixated? Are you a high school or college student who doesn't know what to do with your life yet? Have you just recently lost someone close to you? Are you a pastor or other ministry leader unclear about your calling? Is there a relationship that is broken? Have you been diagnosed with a chronic illness or terminal disease? Maybe it is just that the demands at work are more than you think you can continue to handle. Perhaps it is adjusting to having an empty nest. It could be that you are struggling to come to terms with the reality that you don't feel or look as young as you once did.

Whatever the unique facts of your own story, the road you are on now may feel overwhelming and uncertain. Adjust your gaze; refocus your soul. This is part of the journey through the mystery to growth and development into not just a more informed or wiser person but into a deeper person.

Chapter 3

IS IT KARMA?

What goes around comes around, right? At least that is the life philosophy of Earl Hickey. Television sitcom fans may immediately think of the man whose name is Earl when they hear the word "karma." *My Name Is Earl* traces the up and down journey of its main character as he tries to get rid of all his bad karma. Earl figures if he can make right all the wrong things he has done over his life he can bring about ongoing good fortune for himself.

Earl works from a list he has created that catalogues all his missteps that need to be corrected so bad things don't come his way. He lives by the credo that the good or bad fortune he is experiencing today is the result of the good or bad he has done in the past; therefore, he can create a good future for himself by doing good things today.

Karma is a teaching of the eastern religions of Buddhism and Hinduism in which everything that happens is always connected to and because of some previous evil or good. Consequently, everyone gets what he or she deserves. If you are experiencing difficulty or struggle of some kind, you only brought it on yourself.

Karma isn't just found in Buddhism, Hinduism, and related religious systems. Though not part of orthodox Christian doctrinal construct or biblical revelation, something akin to karma is found in the theology of many Christians. The relationship of sin and suffering is viewed very much in terms of cause and effect. During a dark season of life, the "why" many times at some point takes on the form of "what did I do to deserve this." Some Christians become morbidly introspective about trying to find the evil they must have in their lives to bring about the struggle in which they find themselves—often times to the point of exasperating their struggle.

A strict correspondence of sin and suffering seems to sound biblical. "You may be sure that your sin will find you out." (Numbers 32:23) "A man reaps what he sows." (Galatians 6:7) But our approach to the Scriptures as though they are a repository of propositions that can be lifted out of the narrative and have a meaning on their own and that is universal standing alone apart from the text has gotten us into trouble. It has led us to develop theologies regarding the relationship of sin and suffering that cut right across the grain of two words that are absolutely central to who God is and to what Christian faith is all about—grace and mercy.

Simply put, grace is receiving benefit that we don't deserve; mercy is not receiving punishment that we do deserve. This seems like a complete one-eighty from reaping what we sow and our sins finding us out. Obviously, the relationship of sin and suffering is much more nuanced than indiscriminate cause and effect.

The practical theology of Job's three friends rested upon the basic premise that God sends happiness in proportion to obedience and faithfulness to Him and that He sends trouble in proportion to disobedience and unfaithfulness to Him. This was their jumping off point in their quest to find the answer for why Job found himself where he had. They could only contemplate that there had to be a humanly reasonable cause for Job's plight. The only thing which could fit this parameter was that Job had to have run afoul of God somewhere along the line.

Eliphaz:
"But now trouble comes to you, and you are discouraged; it strikes you, and you are dismayed. Should not your piety be your confidence and your blameless ways your hope? Consider now: Who, being innocent, has ever perished? Where were the upright ever destroyed? As I have observed, those who plow evil and those who sow trouble reap it. At the breath of God they are destroyed; at the blast of his anger they perish." (Job 4:5-9)

Bildad:
"Does God pervert justice? Does the Almighty pervert what is right? When your children sinned against him, he gave them over to the penalty of their sin. But if you will look to God and plead with the Almighty, if you are pure and upright, even now he will rouse himself on your behalf and restore you to your rightful place. Your beginnings will seem humble, so prosperous will your future be." (Job 8:3-7)

Zophar:
"If you put away the sin that is in your hand and allow no evil to dwell in your tent, then you will lift up your face without shame; you will stand firm and without fear. You will surely forget your trouble, recalling it only as waters gone by. Life will be brighter than noonday, and darkness will become like morning." (Job 11:14-17)

We'll see in succeeding chapters three faulty trajectories of reasoning based upon the particular biases of Eliphaz, Bildad, and Zophar. Their respective answers were disastrous. Rather than comfort their friend, they added to his suffering. Instead of helping him lean into God and live in the mystery, they forced him into a self-justifying defense that made the mystery feel like distance between him and God rather than a means to intimacy with God. And it all goes back to their premise, back to their karmic theology. This is the initial step for them toward a wrong destination.

Sports have always been part of life in the Weidman household. Many of our evening meals were scheduled around practices and games while our children were growing up. Paul was involved every year in football and baseball. He also worked in a couple of years each of basketball and track along the way. Adrean played soccer for two years, but her real love was, and still is, softball.

There were times when I would be at one of the kids' games, and Buffy would be at a game of the other. One evening when we were both at our daughter's softball game we had the privilege to spend a fair amount of time talking with the mother of one of the other girls on the team whom, up until that time, we had not gotten to know. We talked about a whole range of things from the yellow LIVESTRONG bracelets to her work as a photo journalist.

Our conversation turned at one point to the confusing layout of streets in many of the Levittown neighborhoods. The only thing that makes sense about the streets in most of those developments is the first letter of the name given them. Levittown, Pennsylvania and neighboring Fairless Hills are communities of thousands of homes that were developed during a period of a few years in the early and mid-1950s. A distinctive feature of most of the developments that comprise Levittown is that all the streets within a particular development begin with the same letter, which corresponds with the first letter of the name of the development. For example, the Pinewood development consists of streets named Pebble Lane, Park Lane, Primrose Lane, etc.

Another distinctive feature of these developments has to do with the vision of the developer and the time period in which they were built. High density neighborhoods prior to that time were generally laid out in linear fashion creating the city block as we know it. A different philosophy guided the initial surge of suburban sprawl that occurred after World War II. Neighborhood streets would be less uniform with curves and houses set back a bit from the curb.

The difference is well seen in aerial photographs or on street maps. Neighborhoods in nearby Philadelphia appear as a collection of rectangles and squares. Levittown developments look more like one maze after another. Driving in them can feel like you are in a maze too.

I got my first taste of how confusing the street layout could be in those developments shortly after our family moved to the Levittown area when I became the pastor of a church there. I went to visit in the home of a family in the church. My adventure began when I turned at the sign to enter their development. For starters, I should have turned at the second entrance to the development; I had taken the first. From that point I was the proverbial mouse trying to find the cheese. I eventually found their house, about 10 or 15 minutes late and by accident.

The photo journalist with whom Buffy and I talked while watching our daughter's softball game had her own initiation by a Levittown maze. She told us the story of getting lost in her own development while taking a walk shortly after moving there. One of the features of some of the developments, as in hers, is a street that encircles the outer perimeter of the development. The maze of other streets is inside the circle. Some streets don't intersect with the circle; others intersect with the circle at a T on both ends of the street. If you turn the wrong direction at one of those T intersections (which is easy to do since it depends upon which end of the street you are on), you can end up going the long way around on the circle. That's what happened to the photo journalist as she walked her new community that day.

Being new to the development, she wasn't aware of the mistake until she found herself at the wrong end of the development from where she really was headed.

Life is far more like the maze of streets in those Levittown developments than neatly aligned squares and rectangles of parallel and perpendicular city streets. So often we try to navigate the maze according to a theological road map that is laid out in neatly aligned blocks. It just doesn't work.

Further, the cause and effect formula in approaching the relationship of sin and suffering is like saying that at a particular intersection you should turn left. But what if you are at the other end of a street that intersects in two places with the circle running around your existence? The left turn will take you absolutely in the wrong direction.

NO SIMPLE ANSWER

Job's friends hung a left with regard to his suffering and ended up in the wrong place. They were locked into the limited mindset that believes suffering proves the displeasure of God and prosperity proves the blessing of God. But it is not that simple.

There is not necessarily a direct correlation between sin and suffering. Job's dark valley of grief and pain is a primary exhibit of this reality. Remember what God declared at the initiation of this season of Job's life. It was not a declaration of His displeasure with Job or about Job's sinfulness but about the uprightness of Job. This was not about Job's karma; it was about God's glory. It was not a case of cause and effect. Job's sins were not finding him out. He was not reaping what he had sown.

Like Job's friends, Jesus' disciples viewed sin and suffering strictly in terms of cause and effect. "As he went along, he saw a man blind from birth. His disciples asked him, 'Rabbi, who sinned, this man or his parents, that he was born blind?'" (John 9:1-2)

They assumed a direct correlation between sin and suffering. So rather than live in the mystery, they proposed what they thought to be the simple answer.

Jesus revealed the narrowness of their theology. "Neither this man nor his parents sinned." (John 9:3)

We know Jesus wasn't teaching that the man and his parents were sinless. A loud and clear message of the Scriptures is that we are all sinners. So what was Jesus talking about when He said that neither the man nor his parents sinned? He was saying that the man's blindness was not the result of sin on their part.

Jesus' disciples had a narrow, dogmatic theology of suffering that needed to be corrected. So did Job's friends. What about us? Where does our theology of suffering need to reflect more humility? Does it allow for the fact that suffering doesn't necessarily prove sinfulness or God's displeasure? Can it leave room for the reality that we don't have all the answers when it comes to the reasons behind our experiences of pain?

CONSEQUENCES

Most every young boy at some point has a friend, brother, cousin, or father who teaches him how to skip rocks across water. I first learned how to skip rocks at a pond on the property of a couple who attended the first church my dad pastored. It was such fun as a kid seeing how many skips you could get. Two or three was common, but there were those few times when the rock seemed to just glide across the water and the number of skips was impossible to count. Even as an adult, I have had a couple of experiences when my wife has had to drag me away from the water's edge because I was so transfixed with skipping rocks.

As great as the exhilaration of sending a rock dancing across the surface of the water, there is an equally deflating experience when the rock just hits the water and immediately plunges beneath the surface with a splash. But then that can become a game. Instead of skipping rocks to see how many jumps off the water you can get, the game is now about seeing how big a splash you can make, but more importantly how far out you can see a discernible ripple. Each rock creates a unique splash and sound. Each also creates a unique ripple. The ripples vary in size and spread as well as direction. In any case, there are ripples when a rock hits the water.

We are in error to think of sin and suffering as having a directly correlated cause and effect relationship. But we would be equally in error to think that sin doesn't have consequences. Those consequences are much like the ripples sent out across the water by a stone. Yes, we who are followers of Jesus Christ need to put away our karma-like theologies that see some kind of cosmic/divine retribution that proportionally and certainly follows each act of sin. At the same time, we must be careful that we do not adopt an essentially hedonistic theology regarding sin—one which says that I can do pretty much what I want because God is forgiving, gracious, and merciful. Sure, He is all of those. He graciously and mercifully forgives us, but sin does have its consequences.

That being said, we need to properly understand the nature of sin's consequences. Otherwise, we can easily end up right back at a theology of karma via cosmic/divine retribution. Many Christians go about life afraid of what God is going to do to them to even the score for what they have done wrong. They know God is loving, gracious, and merciful, but looming larger in their concept of God than these characteristics is a vengeful, wrathful, punishing God.

One passage of Scripture that has been used by some preachers and teachers to keep people on the straight and narrow, and thus has reinforced this warped concept of God, is found in the book of Exodus.

> Then the Lord came down in the cloud and stood there with him and proclaimed his name, the Lord. And he passed in front of Moses, proclaiming, "The Lord, the Lord, the compassionate and gracious God, slow to anger, abounding in love and faithfulness, maintaining love to thousands, and forgiving wickedness, rebellion and sin. Yet he does not leave the guilty unpunished; he punishes the children and their children for the sin of the fathers to the third and fourth generation." (Exodus 34:5-7)

This passage often gets taught with most or all of the emphasis on punishment. God ends up being portrayed in such teaching as one who would be nice to us if we just wouldn't sin and as one who loses His cool when we do sin taking out His anger not only on us but our children and grandchildren like some kind of deranged, abusive father.

Most who take the "sinners in the hands of an angry God" approach to this passage are well-intentioned. They wish the best for those they teach. They would hate to see someone derailed spiritually by the creep of sin in their lives. They simply desire to sound a warning. But in doing so, they prompt people to pursue sin management out of fear rather than to pursue holiness out of love. The former actually causes people to draw back from God; the latter moves people toward God.

Notice in the passage how God takes great pains to declare His love and care for His people before sounding His warning. He goes over the top to make the point that those who live in relationship with Him should have nothing of which to be afraid in Him. Yet there is the warning, and one that on the surface is a bit confounding. So what are we to make of this apparent other side of God that seems to stand ready to visit retribution on any of us who step out of line, and not only on us but also on our kids and grandkids for our bad acts?

The word "punish" in English has come to be so associated with inflicting retribution that it distorts our understanding of what God is really saying in Exodus 34:7. The Hebrew sense of "punish" as used in this verse includes the idea that a penalty for corrective (not retributive) purposes may be imposed. The emphasis is different than the way we in western culture often think of the term. Correction is different than retribution.

There is something even more, though, to the Hebrew concept expressed in the word that is translated "punish." It carries with it the idea of allowing things to run their course. This is the real message God is communicating. He is in effect saying, "If you sin, I will allow the ripple effects of your actions run their course. At times I might even bring some pain or loss into your life not to hurt you, but to get you back on track. I really love you and want to be kind to you, but that doesn't mean I'll jump in and stop the consequences that may come your way or the way of your family."

God is warning us about presuming upon His kindness. He's letting us know that sin has a ripple effect, and that if we choose into it, He will let the ripples happen. If I drive drunk and get into an accident, I am experiencing the ripple effect of my actions. If someone is promiscuous and gets an STD, this is the ripple effect at work. If someone foolishly manages their money resulting in a poor credit score, that is a ripple effect of the person's actions.

The ripple effect of sin, though, should not be thought of as having a predictable pattern of direct correlations. The consequences of sin are often unpredictable just like the varied patterns created when a rock breaks the surface of the water on a pond. Even the same sin results in varied impact in different people's lives because every context is different. It's like two rocks of the same size and shape each being thrown into the water. One is thrown at a low angle and may even skip off the water once or twice before plunging beneath the surface. Very little ripple is created and it goes all in one direction. The other rock is thrown nearly straight up, high into the air and violently bursts through the water surface. It sends up a splash and sends out ripples evenly in every direction that seem to go on and on in ever widening circles.

This ripple effect understanding of the word "punish" in Exodus 34 serves to further amplify the faultiness of a theology in which God sends happiness in proportion to righteousness and trouble in proportion to sinfulness.

So what about this matter of the sin of the fathers being visited upon succeeding generations? Its application is two-fold.

First, we are reminded that the ripple effect of my sin doesn't always just ripple across my life. It can also cause pain and loss to others who are innocent, as in the case of a drunk driver hitting another car or a pedestrian. Second, we are brought to the awareness that the patterns of my behavior ripple across the lives of my children and grandchildren. Not only may they be innocent bystanders impacted by the effects of my actions, but also the patterns of my behavior by way of modeling ripple into their lives as they pick up those patterns themselves. In effect, I train them how to sin in particular ways, which exposes them to the ripple of resulting pain and loss connected to their actions. And so on and so on.

Because sin does have its consequences, we shouldn't rule out sin being a possible cause of suffering. Dark seasons provoke us to look inward, to examine our souls. While we are there in the place of introspection, one of the questions Job asked of God is a good one for us to ask as well: "If I have sinned, what have I done to you, O watcher of men?" (Job 7:20) It is a good time to discover if we are in a period of correction or if we are simply being touched by the ripples of our actions.

Job begins with a good question, but steers off course with a second question that assumes a cosmic/divine retribution is in action. "Why have you made me your target?" (Job 7:20)

It is very likely he was pushed by the attack of his friend Eliphaz into wondering if indeed God were after him. Even as we rightly do some introspection and self-examination, it is important not to be forced by the condemning voices of others (or of ourselves) into thinking God must be exacting retribution upon us for something we have done. Though sin is sometimes the cause of our suffering, God is never out to get us.

THE PARADOX OF GOD'S GOODNESS

Sometimes pain has nothing to do with sin in our lives. The ripples we see in the form of pain, loss, or discomfort are not because of a thrown rock. A lake's surface can be stirred as the wind blows or as a fish jumps. The rolling water may also be the wake of a boat. The struggles of life as well have various sources. Some we can identify; others are a mystery. And as strange as it may sound, one of the sources of hardship is the goodness of God.

We struggle with the paradox that some of life's pains are about God simply being a good Father. Again, this is because we have drawn straight lines between sin and suffering, between righteousness and prosperity. The strangeness of this paradox is further compounded because we have confined expressions of goodness inside of a box called pampering. Western culture places such a premium on ever increasing comfort and convenience that we can hardly get our minds around such a strange concept as hardship being the result of the goodness of God.

The theological and cultural narrowness of Eliphaz, Bildad, and Zophar blinded them to this strange yet wonderful paradox as well. In all of their diatribes against Job, they could not (or would not) conceive of anything of the goodness of God being at work in Job's suffering. Their straight lines were drawn; they were inside their box; and they were dead wrong (Job 42:7).

Let's unstraighten the lines and open the box lid of our narrow theological and cultural premises by allowing paradox and contradiction to be part of the way we understand things to be. The goodness of God can be right at the center of a season of suffering. Much of how that works is hidden in mystery, but there are two expressions of the paradox of God's goodness into which we can have some glimpses of understanding.

First, pain may be discipline that is for our good. Scripture says, "Endure hardship as discipline; God is treating you as sons. For what son is not disciplined by his father? ...God disciplines us for our good." (Hebrews 12:7,10) Too long this has been misunderstood. God's discipline is viewed negatively. It is equated with retributional punishment as was discussed earlier. And even when it isn't understood or presented that way, God's discipline is invariably seen as the result of wrong doing or a misstep on our behalf.

Certainly, God's discipline is sometimes corrective in nature. In these cases, its purpose is to redirect us away from something that is harmful to our relationship with Him, to ourselves, or to others around us. The goal isn't pain; pain is a means to the goal—our good. Therefore, the pain is measured; it is tempered by love.

There are some kids who just won't ever get their homework done if they start watching television after school. Their parents may decide to institute a "no television until homework is done" rule. The kids might complain and argue that it isn't fair or that they are being deprived of enjoyment after a long, hard day at school.

Their parents may say, "If you need a little break after school, you can ride your bike or shoot hoops for a half hour, or you can help me start getting dinner ready. But no TV." This is a corrective act of discipline on the parents' part. From the kids' perspective, there is an experience of pain—no television, but it is actually an expression of goodness by the parents. This is an illustration of the corrective discipline of God.

God's discipline, though, is not merely a corrective act. Sometimes it is, but often it is a formative process. We've all heard the expression "no pain, no gain." It is often used in connection with exercise, but the concept applies to a variety of areas of life in which discipline leads to something good. While the "no TV after school" rule may be initially instituted as a corrective measure, it is likely maintained as a formative discipline.

Many children grow up doing chores. It was no different for me. I was required to do a variety of household chores—vacuuming, washing dishes, dusting, etc.—on a rotating basis with my siblings. In addition, we always had to help with weeding the garden and harvesting its produce. I especially hated shelling peas and lima beans, not only because it was tedious work but also because I hated the taste of both vegetables.

We usually don't refer to things like this as our parents disciplining us, but in all reality that's what they were doing. And I for one am extremely grateful now that mine did so. At the time I thought they were inflicting unfair hardships on me, but without it I wouldn't know how to work alongside my wife making meals and cleaning the house or how to persevere in an unpleasant, but necessary task. Formative discipline was at least as important, if not more important, than the corrective forms of discipline my parents used. It shaped me for adulthood.

God loves us too much to let us remain spiritually immature and flabby. He works from His place of infinite wisdom and understanding to shape our lives and form us into something better than we have been. It is an expression of goodness for Him to do so.

God's goodness expressed in our pain comes not just in the form of corrective or formative discipline. Pain may also be an experience of good being withheld now so we can have something even better later. God is not in the business of pampering us, but He does love to bring joy into our lives. "Every good and perfect gift is from above, coming down from the Father of the heavenly lights." (James 1:17) And He "richly provides us with everything for our enjoyment." (1 Timothy 6:17) God's heart is filled to overflowing with delight when one of His children is reveling over a gift He has given them. We who are human parents experience a bit of what He feels as we see the eyes of our children open wide with sheer joy and wonderment when opening a Christmas or birthday gift or when encountering an awesome surprise.

Our son, Paul, began rooting for the Philadelphia Eagles as soon as he was old enough to understand a little bit of what was going on as he watched football games with me. The Penn State Nittany Lions emerged as his favorite college football team at that time as well. When he was still a preschooler, I remember how excited I was for him when I took home tickets I had purchased for a Penn State football game from a season ticket holder who couldn't go to the game that particular week. We still have a picture of Paul holding up those tickets as we left early in the morning for the game.

Penn State football tickets are quite difficult to come by, but I had the chance to take Paul to two games by the time he was in kindergarten. However, we had not ever been to an Eagles game, something he would have loved to do. Then, when he was in third grade, our family moved to a suburb just outside of Philadelphia. Buffy and I weren't sure how the kids would take it when we announced to them we would be moving, particularly since it was the middle of the school year.

Paul's immediate reaction was, "Great! Can we get Eagles tickets?"

We moved right at the end of the season so attending a game that year wasn't a possibility. Procuring Eagles tickets went on the back burner until the next summer. I hadn't yet found out whether I would be able to buy tickets to a game or two that upcoming season when an idea came to me one Saturday morning. Training camp was underway, and there was a scrimmage that afternoon with the Buffalo Bills. My idea was to take Paul to the scrimmage just in case I couldn't get tickets to any games that year.

The Eagles hold summer training camp at Lehigh University in Bethlehem, Pennsylvania about an hour from Philadelphia. So we would have a little drive ahead of us that morning. Before telling Paul where we were going, my plan developed further. I decided not to tell him where we were headed, and to let it be a wonderful surprise when we arrived at the Eagles' training facility.

My wife and daughter had something going on that morning so it gave me the perfect set up. After Paul finished breakfast, I told him, "Paul, I've had something come up at the last minute just this morning, and I have to go somewhere. Because mom and Adrean won't be around, you'll have to come with me."

Paul wanted to know how long it would take. After all there were Saturday morning cartoons and other kid things to do. I told him that the place I had to go was about an hour away and that I was so sorry it was ruining his Saturday morning. I told him I would be sure to have us do something fun together that afternoon.

He seemed satisfied with that and didn't really ask any more questions about where we were going. I think he just assumed this had something to do with my work as a pastor. Even as we drove along together, he seemed relatively unconcerned about the mystery of this trip. However, he was bored (as is the case with about any nine-year old in the car for more than fifteen or twenty minutes) and would have much preferred doing something else on a Saturday morning. Though he didn't complain too much, this was a pain for him.

Several miles from the Eagles training facility, we approached the interchange of two highways where I needed to exit. Paul read the sign that pointed the way toward Bethlehem. He asked me, "Bethlehem? Isn't that where Lehigh is, where the Eagles have training camp?"

I answered, still not revealing our destination, "It sure is."

He then added, "Did you know the Eagles have a scrimmage today with the Buffalo Bills?"

I could hardly contain my excitement so as not to ruin the surprise. "I think I saw something about that on the news last night."

The subject changed, and we drove on.

We arrived at the exit for Lehigh University. As I drove down the exit ramp, Paul asked, "Is your meeting near Lehigh?"

I told him, "Yeah, pretty close."

I think he was consoling himself with the idea that even though his Saturday morning was ruined at least he got to be near where the Eagles were practicing.

The road leading past the practice facility started to back up with traffic. Paul commented that it must be from people coming to see the scrimmage. I mumbled something about hoping I wouldn't be late for my meeting. This was to keep the surprise concealed as long as possible.

We were coming up on the last turn to go to the training facility when Paul asked me, "How long will your meeting take?"

As I turned in the same direction as all the other traffic heading toward Eagles camp in accordance with the sign at the intersection, I answered him by saying, "Well, how long do you think the scrimmage will be?"

Paul's face told the whole story about how his mind was working to grasp what was really happening. Could it be true? Surely it has to be. But maybe it isn't.

Then the words came with hopeful anticipation, "Are we going to the Eagles scrimmage?"

Telling him "yes" ranks among some of my favorite moments during his childhood. We had a great time that day. And by the way, we did get tickets to a couple of regular season games that year.

The joy Paul experienced that day was heightened because of the way it came. He had to travel a mysterious, and not very pleasant, journey. He missed out on the happy pursuits of a nine-year old on a Saturday morning. Sure, he would have been excited and we would have had fun if I had simply sprung on him the news of where we were going at the very outset of that morning. But there was something so much more amazing for him and for me as a result of the way we got to that destination.

I can't help but to think of the call of Abram in the Old Testament as I reflect on what Paul experienced that Saturday morning in the summer of 1998 and how it illustrates what it is to live in the mystery.

> The Lord had said to Abram, "Leave your country, your people and your father's household and go to the land I will show you. …So Abram left, as the Lord had told him…" (Genesis 12:1,4)

Abram doesn't know where he is going. He doesn't know how to get there. But he is going. He is on a mysterious journey to an unknown place. How does he even know if he is going in the right direction? How will he know when he gets there? How is this all going to turn out?

Sometimes the plot lines of our lives twist in such a way that we end up in a season that feels like we are on a trip without directions to a still to be disclosed destination. We feel like we are leaving the known and familiar for the unknown and un-familiar. We sense loss in not being in a more preferable place and the unpleasantness of just not knowing.

The goodness of God is at work there. We may not feel the tangible result of it. In fact, that goodness touching us in a tangible way is actually being held back. But that holding back is not a lack of goodness, it is a storing up of goodness for a later and greater manifestation. The goodness of God doesn't cease during the holding back of its temporal manifestation; it simply is shrouded from our view by the veil of mystery surrounding it. But when it bursts forth from behind the veil and the look on our face tells the story of how our mind is trying to grasp the wonder of the moment, God's heart is full, and we experience how truly good His goodness is.

This was the case for the blind man who Jesus healed in John 9, which was referenced earlier in this chapter. After dispelling the disciples' karma-like theology regarding the man's suffering, Jesus declared the paradox of God's goodness: "This happened so that the work of God might be displayed in his life." (John 9:3)

Each day the man spent in darkness was increasing the joy that was going to be felt when he would declare, "One thing I do know. I was blind and now I see." (John 9:25) It was building up to a grand crescendo when he would meet the Savior and have his life transformed, not just in his physical eyes but also in the depths of his soul and spirit (John 9:35-38).

Living in the mystery sometimes feels like we are walking around blind. A season of darkness that has enveloped our existence leaves us uncertain about whether we are going in the right direction and anxious about how things will turn out. But in the darkness, hidden from view for now, is always the goodness of God.

There are those times when goodness is hidden from view by the mystery. Yet it is still there leading toward a great unveiling somewhere down the road that will bring great joy to our hearts and to God's as well.

Chapter 4

TRADITIONALISM'S
PRESUMPTIVE ANSWERS

Phillip McGraw, better known as Dr. Phil, rose meteorically to fame in the late 1990s and early 2000s for his straight talking advice. His big break came when he made an appearance on the *Oprah Winfrey Show*. If Oprah liked you, it was golden. And she loved Phil McGraw. He was a regular on her program before he secured his own daytime talk show.

His television program was in the line of the age old newspaper or magazine advice column. Celebrity advisors for life's issues like child rearing, sex, office etiquette, household cleaning tips, and more have been a staple of American popular culture for the last half century or so.

Besides turning to Dr. Phil or some other well-known advisor, we frequently turn to our friends, family, and co-workers for answers to our problems in life. The conversation begins with the simple phrase, "Can I get your advice about something?" Sometimes, we also get their advice when we haven't even asked for it.

It's very easy to find people willing and ready to give us answers, and aren't we often eager ourselves to provide answers to others. Generally, we work from the framework that questions are things to be answered rather than things to cause us to think and that raise more questions. We are empirically minded problem solvers in western culture. Mystery is not something with which we interact well.

I'm not making a case against seeking advice. Wise people seek counsel when they are faced with challenging decisions and circumstances. The Scriptures tell us this much. "Listen to advice and accept instruction, and in the end you will be wise." (Proverbs 19:20) Good counsel provides another perspective and insights from another point of view that can broaden our understanding.

Not all of the answers we get and give is very good counsel though. Much of what passes for advice, not only what we receive but also what we dispense, are just clichés and pop psychology mixed with our own biases. It may sound wise and good on the surface, but often it is quite disconnected from the reality of the situation into which it tries to speak.

This was the problem with Job's three friends. They had their nice, clean, neat theologies with the accompanying clichés and biases. They tried to speak into Job's situation from their preconceptions and with their prepackaged answers, and they completely missed the mark. Each friend and his attempt to provide an answer for Job's suffering makes for an interesting study into three typical approaches of practical (or should I say impractical) theology of many Christians today. These are three ways of trying to make sense of mystery, of trying to answer the question "Why?" But each are found wanting; they are answers that do not cut it for so many of our toughest trials.

The first of Job's friends to speak was Eliphaz. The culture of that day tells us he would have been the oldest since he spoke first. The other friends deferred to his counsel being offered before theirs since he had more experience and presumably more wisdom. This turns out to be the basis of his appeal to Job—experience and wisdom (really conventional wisdom). Traditionalism was his biased perspective. We'll see that his approach, like so many today, is limited and presumptive.

BEING TOO SURE OF THINGS

I was at a conference in Sacramento, California a number of years ago when my cell phone rang. A meeting of which I was a part had just finished, and I was beginning to work with two others from the meeting to write a report that would be submitted the next day of the conference. My wife's cell phone number came up on the display. As I pressed the talk button on my phone, I assumed this was another call checking in just to tell each other how much we missed and loved each other. I could simply tell her that I would call her back later since I had important work to do.

Her first sentence was not, "Hey, how it's going. I was thinking about you, so I thought I would call."

Instead, Buffy informed me, "I've got a big problem with the car and need you to help me figure out what to do."

At this point, I was thinking, "I'm 3,000 miles away. What do you expect me to do from here?" Trying not to be impatient, though, I asked, "What's the problem?"

Buffy described to me that she had dropped off Adrean at softball practice and then taken our son Paul to his baseball game. She stayed to watch some of the game before she needed to go pick up Adrean from practice. When Buffy tried to start the car to go get our daughter, she couldn't turn the key in the ignition. A friend of ours happened to be there and tried to help her figure out what may have been going on, but to no avail. He wanted to know if there was some kind of ignition release that had to be pressed to allow the key to turn. But our car didn't have such a device.

I interrupted and said, "Oh, I know what's going on. This has happened to me before. Just turn the wheel while trying to turn the key."

The steering column lock safety feature that is in most every car can sometimes get stuck. It happened to be that it occurred with some degree of frequency in this particular car. Apparently, Buffy hadn't had it happen to her and didn't know how to get it unstuck.

She tried what I asked as I impatiently looked at my watch and then over to the others with whom I had to write the report. No success. Her frustration was rising and so was mine, each for very different reasons. Her concern was centered on the East Coast and with being late for picking up Adrean. Mine was on the West Coast and with keeping my colleagues waiting.

"Do it again," I said, "sometimes it takes a couple of tries."

Nothing.

I proceeded to tell her that she must be doing it wrong, because it always works for me. She, then, had our friend try to unlock the steering wheel and ignition.

Again, no luck. Buffy suggested that maybe something else was wrong with the car.

It is probably a good thing I was 3,000 miles away, because what I said next deserved to get me slapped up side of the head by my wife. "I'm sure that's what is wrong. You guys have got to be working the steering wheel and ignition incorrectly."

There were a few more tense words with each other before we settled on Buffy arranging to have the car towed to our mechanic. The frustration of knowing we would incur an unnecessary towing expense prompted me to add, "Once it gets to the mechanic you'll find out that the problem is what I said it is."

We talked on the phone again later that night largely avoiding mention of the situation with the car, mostly because we didn't want to argue. Instead, this was a conversation about the rest of what happened in ours and the kids' day and a chance to say "good-night" and "I love you."

The next afternoon my cell phone rang. It was Buffy. I began anticipating the words which would confirm what I had been so sure of the day before.

"Hey, Buffy how's it going today," I said, ready for news about the car.

"Not bad. The mechanic called, and the ignition switch was bad," she replied.

Needless to say, I did a fair amount of apologizing for my arrogant assuredness of the day before.

Being too sure of things limits our perspective. This was my problem that afternoon in Sacramento. I relied so heavily on my experience that I presumed things to be a certain way, when in reality they were not. I was so sure of how things were that I ruled out any other possible explanations. Rather than reflect humble confidence, I demonstrated arrogant certainty. Consequently, I was of little or no help to my wife. In fact, I frustrated her in an already frustrating situation.

Eliphaz did the same thing in his approach to Job's situation. He cited prior experience and used it as a foundation upon which he built his certitude about sin being the cause of Job's suffering.

"As I have observed, those who plow evil and those who sow trouble reap it. ...I myself have seen a fool taking root, but suddenly his house was cursed." (Job 4:8; 5:3)

He didn't consider another possibility, because he was so sure he had this thing all figured out. After all, he had been around a lot longer than anyone sitting in that ash heap. He should know. Right? But he didn't know.

Job had open hands in this place of mystery. He left open the possibility that maybe there had been sin in his life for which God was trying to correctively discipline him. He didn't think so, but he wasn't going to be so sure that he ruled out the possibility.

He did, however, in his openness to maybe being wrong, uncover the arrogant certitude of Eliphaz. "Teach me, and I will be quiet, show me where I have been wrong. How painful are honest words! But what do your arguments prove?" (Job 6:24-25)

Job put his finger on the problem with Eliphaz's approach. Eliphaz took the position that his experience told him Job had to have sinned because of the great suffering he was experiencing. Job challenged that presumption by asking Eliphaz to tell him the specific sin of which he was guilty. Job would gladly have confessed it if there had been some sin, but Eliphaz couldn't point any out. His certainty wasn't based on actual reality or fact but upon a conventional wisdom born out of assumptions.

It was Socrates who said "The only true wisdom is in knowing you know nothing." He is also attributed with saying, "Wisdom begins in wonder."

Mystery by its very definition is a place of wonder, of not knowing. Yet there will be people who are sure they have the answer for our season of darkness. It will come by way of well-meaning advice that expresses a limited perspective on our situation. It will present itself as wise experience, but in reality it is fairly shallow, the assumptions of a know-it-all.

Experience is valuable to inform our understanding of the world, and it teaches us many things. But experience doesn't mean that we have some kind of corner on the truth. There will always be much about which we just don't know. There will always be things experience will not prepare us to understand.

HAVING KNOWLEDGE WITHOUT INSIGHT

One of the things the presumptive traditionalist is really sure about is that he or she is in the know. They have been well informed through a variety of experiences, and armed with their knowledge and logic and facts, they are ready to solve your problem and mine. Any suggestion that they might not know what they are talking about is an offense to them. They would retort that they have forgotten more than we ever learned, especially if we are younger and less experienced than they.

This was Eliphaz. As he heard Job question the logic of him and the other two friends and declare his integrity in spite of their charges of wrong-doing, Eliphaz was put off. His traditional assumptions were questioned, and he wouldn't stand for that. In his mind, he knew better than Job. To him, what did this young pup know?

"Do you listen to God's counsel? Do you limit wisdom to yourself? What do you know that we do not know? What insights do you have that we do not have? The gray-haired and the aged are on our side, men even older than your father.

"...Listen to me and I will explain to you; let me tell you
what I have seen, what wise men have declared, hiding
nothing received from their fathers..." (Job 15:8-10,17-18)

Eliphaz was informed by the traditions and collective understanding passed down from prior generations; he himself had
lived and learned. For all of his knowledge, though, he lacked
insight to see that Job's situation was beyond him and his
understanding.

Job was bludgeoned with cold, hard information and logic
(which were irrelevant to his situation anyway), but was shown
no sympathy and care. Facts without feelings became additional
arrows to his wounded soul.

"Will your long-winded speeches never end? What ails
you that you keep on arguing? I also could speak like you, if
you were in my place; I could make fine speeches against you
and shake my head at you. But my mouth would encourage
you; comfort from my lips would bring you relief."
(Job 16:3-5)

Having knowledge without insight limits our empathy. It
makes us about as caring as a computer.

A computer has what is referred to as artificial intelligence.
Its calculating capacity is tremendous. It processes significant
databases of information. In that sense, it can outthink the
brightest of human minds.

A computer is quite limited however. First, it only operates
according to what is programmed into it. While the computing
capability is geometric, it is still *artificial* intelligence.

Another significant limitation of a computer is that it follows
logical sequences of electronic data strings. If the sequence is

broken at any place, the computer can't make sense of the data and stops working properly. Further, that's all a computer does; it follows its programmed logical sequence, but it can't feel.

We've all had those times when our computer pops up a dialogue box notifying us of an error and bleeps at us. I don't know about you, but I almost feel like the computer is swearing at me. And never has that dialogue box said something like, "I realize you've had a long day and that because you're tired you clicked on the wrong place. Don't worry about it. You'll get it right next time. Go ahead; try again. You can do it."

My computer can process a lot of information, but it doesn't have insight, and therefore, it doesn't have empathy. As a result, it couldn't care less whether I've had a long day or not.

Eliphaz along with today's presumptive traditionalists are programmed to think a certain way. This programming has come by way of the input of others who pass along conventional wisdom and knowing clichés. But so much of life, especially the dark seasons, doesn't follow their perfectly coded string of logic. Nuance doesn't compute for them. Though they are certain about their limited perspective, there is no insight, no empathy. Their answers are of little help deep in the fog of mystery.

FOLLOWING DEAD FORMULAS

Traditionalism is about preserving the formula for how something is done and for how the world is interpreted. It is assumed that A plus B must always equal C. Its formulaic approach to life takes what worked in other times and in other situations and forces it into the current reality.

Again, the computer helps us understand the limitations of the answers provided by the presumptive traditionalist. The

Microsoft Excel program is extremely useful for compiling and calculating large volumes of numerical data. The spreadsheet consists of lettered columns and numbered rows that form a table of cells, one cell for each coordinate. For example, A5, G18, D6, etc. are each individual cells in an Excel spreadsheet.

While I've been writing this chapter, I helped my wife develop an Excel spreadsheet to help her efficiently prepare work schedules for the restaurant she manages. It instantaneously calculates each employee's and the whole staff's number of work hours for each day of the week and for the whole week as scheduled times are entered into the appropriate cells.

The cells in the section of the spreadsheet that calculates total hours for individual employees and for the staff each contain mathematical formulas that reference cells in the schedule section of the spreadsheet. Therefore, if a begin time of 10:00 AM and an end time of 3:00 PM is entered on Monday for an employee named Tom, four cells in the hours worked section of the spreadsheet (Tom's hours worked for Monday, Tom's hours worked for the week, total staff hours worked for Monday, and total staff hours worked for the week) reference that data and calculate five hours into their equations.

The formulas in the spreadsheet are nifty tools that will save my wife a lot of time. As well as those formulas work in that particular spreadsheet, it won't be of any help to simply copy and paste them into another spreadsheet that is used to, let's say, track profitability by days of the week and work shifts. I would just get a bunch of error messages because the formulas are dead in that context. They don't connect to the kind of data we're compiling, nor do they correlate to the specific layout in this particular spreadsheet.

The conventional wisdom of the traditionalist is a copy and paste approach to life. What worked over there and back then is plugged into here and now. Not only that, it is expected to work just the same. Just follow the formula and everything is supposed to work out.

Flowing out of Eliphaz's limited theology on suffering came a formula for making Job's pain go away and bringing prosperity back into his life again.

> "Is it for your piety that he rebukes you and brings charges against you? Is not your wickedness great? Are not your sins endless? ...Submit to God and be at peace with him; in this way prosperity will come to you. ...If you return to the Almighty, you will be restored..." (Job 22:4-5,21,23)

Eliphaz did not give Job real hope or true direction to find God amid the senselessness. He only had analysis, only a formula for Job to confess and turn from sin that he didn't have in his life. Eliphaz didn't really understand Job's situation or Job's heart. Following dead formulas limited his helpfulness.

Some Christians today are so beholden to traditions that they live as though life is a formula to be worked out. Do "A;" add to it some "B;" and voila you get "C." They apply these formulas to their own lives as well as try to force these formulas onto others. When mystery comes, the knee jerk reaction is to whip out the formulas that their traditions have formed and interpret the dark season through that grid. This lifeless formulation provides no help, no real hope, no way to a vital connection with God. Thus the struggle of mystery is compounded.

This is not to say that tradition is bad. The issue has to do with our relationship to tradition. Do we relate to tradition as a formula that dictates and binds us? Or do we understand tradetion as a flexible thread that connects us to something larger than ourselves and our own time? As theologians Stanley Grenz and

John Franke put it, "Tradition is comprised by the ongoing deposit of 'wisdom' emerging from [the] dynamic movement of the community under the Spirit's guidance."[3] So tradition, rightly understood and engaged, is not intended to create a static and fixed way of understanding life and being in this world.

Living tradition is set in sharp contrast against dead traditionalism. Eliphaz and those like him in our day drink from the stagnant cistern of dead traditionalism. This was the same well from which the religious leaders of Jesus' day drank, and it was one of the biggest issues He had with them.

Jesus calls us away from dead traditionalism, away from following formulas that are out of date and useless. "Neither do men pour new wine into old wineskins. If they do, the skins will burst, the wine will run out and the wineskins will be ruined. No, they pour new wine into new wineskins, and both are preserved." (Matthew 9:17) He illustrates in the wine and wineskins that for tradition to be of any value we must engage with it in a dynamic, living way.

One of the places in which we are most familiar with dynamic tradition is the big year-end family holidays of Thanksgiving and Christmas. They have become tradition rich celebrations not only of gratefulness for our bounty and of Christ's birth but also of family togetherness. There is much nostalgia connected to that time of the year for many people. Our generation's approach to celebrating has been formed and shaped by the traditions handed down from generations before. We take those timeless traditions, and rather than copying and pasting them into our living rooms and dining rooms we add our own meaningful variations and alternatives.

I am reminded of an attempt when Buffy and I were first married to form our own meaningful version of the time honored tradition of putting up the Christmas tree. As

Christmas approached, we began talking about when we wanted to put up the tree. Would it be Thanksgiving weekend like my mother often liked to do? Would it be Christmas Eve like my grandparents sometimes had practiced? How about early in December like Buffy's family had done?

Thanksgiving seemed too early because we didn't want to be tired of having a tree in our living room by the time Christmas rolled around. Christmas Eve wasn't a viable option either. We wanted to have some time leading up to Christmas to just sit and enjoy looking at the decorated tree.

One of the things we settled on was the fact that a Saturday night or a Sunday afternoon would probably be the best time. I liked Sunday afternoon. We could turn on some football; make some snacks; and get into the Christmas spirit. Now that we decided our tradition would be to put up our Christmas tree on Sunday afternoon, we had to determine which Sunday afternoon. Would it be the Sunday before Christmas or the Sunday after Thanksgiving? Or was there some other Sunday that would be better?

We both liked the idea of doing it about halfway between the first week of December and Christmas. Strange as this may sound, we decided that our Christmas tree tradition would be to put it up on the Sunday afternoon closest to the 15th of December. It seemed to make a lot of sense then, but it put us in the formula trap.

Our Christmas tree tradition worked well for a few years. We had some wonderful Sunday afternoons in those days. But then new realities began to come our way like having children and entering pastoral ministry. Those two factors made Sunday afternoon Christmas decorating a draining chore more than a special celebration.

The way we observed that tradition wasn't working for us anymore. But we tried to keep it going for another year or two—after all this was our tradition and we needed to keep it alive. But in reality, forcing the issue of the Sunday afternoon closest to the 15th of December actually killed the joy and celebration. The tradition had lost its meaning. The formula was dead and proved useless to help us celebrate, reminisce, and enjoy simply being together. Fortunately, we quickly moved our new wine to a new wineskin, and new life was breathed into putting up our Christmas tree.

Some of us are forcing formulas upon the mystery that we or others face. These formulas may even have been birthed out of a rich tradition. The formula in a time and place worked—it had meaning and value. But now it is just a formula, a dead formula, that isn't helping in the mystery. It is only making the mystery more confusing.

It doesn't have to be this way though. We don't have to be frustrated by traditionalism's presumptive answers. We can pour the new wine into a new wineskin. Then tradition can be the flexible thread that weaves into the mystery. Though it may not give us all the answers to the uncertainties of that place, it will help us see that there is a larger context within which the mystery fits and unfolds.

◊ ◊ ◊

There are plenty of Eliphazes running around our churches, neighborhoods, and workplaces. They impose their certain, narrow formula of how things are or should be upon others' uncertain situations.

But God has also gifted us with many wonderful, un-assuming people who don't think they have it all figured out.

They are simply down the road just a little farther than we are. They have experienced some things and have gained some insights into themselves and others, into life itself, and into God. They are willing to share their stories with us. Yet they also see that we have our own unique story.

These truly wise souls listen to our story; they enter into it with us. Their presence makes the hard journey through the uncertainty of mystery a little easier to bear. These are people to be embraced, learned from, and permitted to do life with us. They also become our mentors so you and I can carry on their legacy by becoming a gift in like manner to those who walk the road just a little bit after us.

Chapter 5

LEGALISM'S
GRACELESS ANSWERS

The church of which I was the pastor in the northeastern suburbs of Philadelphia changed its name during the time of my ministry there. We filed an amendment to our Articles of Incorporation with the state of Pennsylvania and received the appropriately stamped document from the government making our new name official. That was actually the easy part. We still had to update the name with all of our vendors, the bank, and others with whom we did business.

There was nothing terribly difficult about this task; it was just time consuming. Most situations simply required that we send a letter or complete a form. A few necessitated providing a copy of the stamped document from the state of Pennsylvania in addition to the letter or form. But there was one matter that was a bit more involved—updating our name on the property deed.

First, we had to get a new deed prepared. An attorney retained by our denomination's district completed the work for us, but since he was halfway across the state, I would need to go to our county courthouse to file the deed after he sent it to me.

A day or two after the deed arrived I had some time in my afternoon schedule to make the drive to the courthouse. It was just over 20 miles to the courthouse, a 45 minute drive if traffic wasn't too heavy. After some quick lunch, I made the trek figuring I could still be back to my office by three o'clock.

I arrived at the courthouse in decent time, rode the elevator to the appropriate floor, and found the office of the Recorder of Deeds. There were a few people waiting, and I took a number to mark my place in line. The line wasn't moving too quickly. I soon realized I would be here longer than expected. But that was okay with me, this needed to be done. It was the last loose end on the name change, and then it would be over.

Finally, my number was called. I stepped up to the counter and informed the woman waiting there for me that I had a deed to file. She took one look at the document and said, "I can't accept this. It's not done correctly."

A little confused, I said, "We had an attorney, who specializes in Pennsylvania real estate law, prepare this deed. What's the problem?"

She was unimpressed and told me, "It isn't in the right format. Our office only accepts deeds that are formatted according to our requirements."

I was handed a document that explains the peculiar, and very specific, way that this particular courthouse wanted deeds to be formatted. It contained things like how much the margins were to be on the page, the way the page headers were supposed to be set up, and other such things that had nothing to do with the actual legal content.

Not too happy that I was on the verge of having an entire afternoon wasted for something that apparently had nothing to do with the legality of this deed, I pushed back a bit. "So, there's nothing wrong with this deed as far as the legal requirements of Pennsylvania?"

"That's not my business; I wouldn't know," she retorted. "I'm just telling you that I won't accept a deed that isn't laid out according to these guidelines."

Clearly, she was not going to budge. There was no room for any give on this. I wasn't going to win this one, so I gave up and went home in great frustration.

The next day I called the attorney to explain what happened. He told me that she really shouldn't have rejected the deed since it met the requirements of state law. Some county Recorder's have preferred formatting and provide guidelines for such to encourage attorneys to submit documents that have a uniform look. These formatting preferences are just that—preferences. But in some instances, a bureaucrat at the counter turns them into a rigid requirement.

The attorney's advice was that we simply reformat the deed to the preference of the county and try again. I sent him the formatting document that I had been given, and a week or two later a reformatted deed arrived in the church mailbox. Nothing had been changed in the actual content of the deed. There was now a little wider margin and a minor realignment on the page header.

After my lunch a day or two later, I once again made the 45 minute trek to the courthouse. I rode up the elevator, went down the hall to the Recorder's office, and took a number. This day there was only one person ahead of me. Shortly, my number was called.

I stepped up to the counter. The woman who took one look at the deed a couple weeks back and immediately rejected it on this day took one look at the slightly reformatted deed and immediately said, "That will be forty-five dollars."

More than a few Christians approach theology and life like the woman at the counter in the Recorder's office approached me trying to file that deed. Preferences are turned into rules and strictly enforced. There is no give, no flex. The rules are the rules. There is no grace, no allowable deviation from the standard that has been imposed.

Job's second friend, Bildad, was one such person. While Eliphaz was overly concerned with conventional wisdom, Bildad was overly concerned with justice. He took a very lawyerly approach to things in life. Everything to him was black and white, no gray areas. He was the quintessential legalist. Like the woman at the counter, like the Pharisees of Jesus' day, and like too many Christians today, Bildad's legalism made him narrow and lacking in grace.

BEING COLDLY RIGID

It is interesting to sit over the wing of an airplane during flight. Among things I've noticed the numerous times I've been in a window seat on the wing is the way the flaps move to assist with takeoff and landing, ascent and descent. Another observation is the way the wing seems to bounce, particularly when there is some turbulence.

There is a certain amount of give, or flex, in the wings of an airplane. They are not absolutely rigid. This wing flexure is necessary to assist with the control and stability of the airplane in flight.

Bildad's theology of God's justice was very rigid. It had no flexure and lacked the ability to move graciously through the turbulence of life. In the abstract, in theory, his theology seems to work, but applied to the real life situation of his friend Job, it just didn't fly. Not only was this graceless legalist narrow and rigid, there was a coldness in his theology that made him sound like a sadist.

"Does God pervert justice? Does the Almighty pervert what is right? When your children sinned against him, he gave them over to the penalty of their sin." (Job 8:3-4)

As far as Bildad was concerned, Job and his kids got what they deserved, and to him that's the way it should be. Job got no sympathy or compassion from Bildad. There was no salve for his wounds, only salt to be rubbed in. The legalist's version of justice was narrow and harsh, rigid and cold.

Being coldly rigid neglects mercy. It is a theology no more bound to fly than a 747 with one wing. The wing of mercy and the wing of justice are both essential to understanding God's interaction with us. He is both just and merciful. "Consider therefore the kindness and sternness of God..." (Romans 11:22) He is always perfectly and infinitely both just and merciful.

If there were only justice, there would be no hope for anyone. There is no one righteous before God. (Psalm 14:1-3; Romans 3:10) That's why we need mercy. Hope is found in God's mercy, not in adherence to religious laws.

No one will be declared righteous in his sight by observing the law; rather, through the law we become conscious of sin. (Romans 3:20)

He saved us, not because of righteous things we had done, but because of his mercy. (Titus 3:5)

Job was hammered mercilessly by Bildad's legalistic, justice driven answers. Though he staggered from yet another verbal punch, something deep inside Job knew that his standing before God was not based upon his good acts, but upon God's mercy.

> But how can a mortal be righteous before God?
> ...Though I were innocent, I could not answer him; I could only plead with my Judge for mercy. (Job 9:2,15)

Job recognized something that we all need to see in ourselves. Even at our best we are still in need of God's mercy.

Bildad worked from a different place though. It was the same premise that drives so much of the ministry service of many Christians today. It functions as if divine favor is found by those who tow the line, follow the rules, and work for God. The legalist proudly touts his wonderful service to the Lord, like the Pharisee in Jesus' parable of Luke 18:9-14, as though he were doing God some kind of favor. Mercy may be a word in the legalist's vocabulary, but it is not a functional part of his life. Therefore, in dealing with others, mercy is neglected.

Those who are acutely aware of their own need of mercy (like Job and like the tax collector who stood in such contrast to the Pharisee in the Luke 18 parable) are also able to be ministers of mercy to others. Jesus said in Luke 6:36, "Be merciful, just as your Father is merciful." He is calling us to pass on the mercy we have experienced. Mercy, not judgment, speaks hope, healing, and help into the struggle with mystery.

MAKING JUDGMENTAL ASSUMPTIONS

One of the greatest gifts to someone in a season of significant or profound mystery is two open ears combined with an open heart. One of the greatest barriers to being able to offer this gift of empathetic listening is jumping to conclusions. When we have an answer before someone is finished talking, we are really not listening; we are formulating assumptions. Often times, these assumptions are incorrect making our counsel worthless, even harmful.

Each of Job's three friends had taken a first round of shots at his character. Then, Eliphaz started up a second round. Wearied, Job presented his case once again. He just needed someone to listen to him. He needed someone to hear his heart. But that gift was withheld.

Bildad jumped in. He had heard enough. He had the solution. To Bildad, if Job would just shut up and take his advice, all would be well.

"When will you end these speeches? Be sensible, and then we can talk. Why are we regarded as cattle and considered stupid in your sight?" (Job 18:2-3)

Bildad was so convinced of the rightness of his outlook on the source of Job's suffering that, though he heard words coming from Job's mouth, he wasn't listening to Job's heart. His one way communication jumped to conclusions and made judgmental assumptions about Job and his relationship to God.

The moment Job most needed to be heard is when Bildad upped the ante. He took the charge against Job to another level. Up to this point, the three friends had urged Job to confess whatever sin must be the cause of his suffering. But now, Bildad called into question whether Job even knew God.

> "Surely such is the dwelling of an evil man; such is the place of one who knows not God."
> (Job 18:21)

If legalists can't win their argument by way of shaming and laying guilt upon the one who doesn't comply with their unbending theology, they simply make a judgment that the person can't truly know God. More than a few followers of Christ have been dubbed "not truly saved" or "heretic" because they didn't dot the "i" or cross the "t" the way a graceless legalist thought they should.

In addition to inflicting pain upon the subject of the legalist's reproach, making judgmental assumptions promotes hypocrisy. The legalist holds others up to a strict code in which loopholes are found for themselves.

I must admit that I am generally not the most grace-filled person when I'm driving, and easily get frustrated (okay... angry) with other drivers. The middle digit doesn't get raised nor do I hang my head out the window hurling profanities, but I do more than my fair share of talking to myself (or my passengers if someone else is riding with me) about how inconsiderate or stupid other drivers happen to be.

One of the things that most irritates me is when I'm gliding along in the passing lane and a car up ahead moves from the other lane to also pass but is moving much slower than I am. It especially pushes my buttons when I have the cruise control set and the other driver doesn't speed up to quickly overtake the car they are passing. This means I have to tap my brakes to kick off the cruise control.

The famous cutoff also gets a rise out of me. It is at times like these that I declare judgment upon my perceived antagonist suggesting everything from the other driver being a jerk to having gotten their license from a cereal box. I'm a Bildad in traffic—an assuming judge, but also a hypocrite.

It's no surprise to you, I am sure, that I too have been guilty of cutting off another driver or not paying attention when the red light turned green. Here is the kicker though. When I'm the offender, I hope for, even expect, a measure of grace to understand that I'm not really a jerk or that my driver's license really did come from the Department of Transportation. I put up my hands as to say "Oops" and mouth "I'm sorry" to the other driver. Sometimes they smile graciously; sometimes they flip me off anyway.

Thomas 'a Kempis had it so right, "How rarely we weigh our neighbor in the same balance in which we weigh ourselves."[4] When all is said and done, there is hypocrisy lurking within every one of us. Making judgmental assumptions is what brings it out.

The more incensed I get over another driver's errors the more it makes me a hypocrite when I make a driving mistake. The more we enforce a code upon another the more we really judge ourselves. Romans 2:1 puts it this way, "You, therefore, have no excuse, you who pass judgment on someone else, for at whatever point you judge the other, you are condemning yourself, because you who pass judgment do the same things."

Job put Bildad's judgmental spirit to the test. Bildad had essentially told Job that he should shut up and listen, that he was just talking too much and not listening enough. Yet that is exactly what Bildad was guilty of doing himself. And not only was he not listening to Job, he was crushing Job's spirit.

"How long will you torment me and crush me with words? Ten times now you have reproached me; shamelessly you attack me.

"If you say, 'How we will hound him, since the root of the trouble lies in him,' you should fear the sword yourselves; for wrath will bring punishment by the sword, and then you will know that there is judgment." (Job 19:2-3,28-29)

If Bildad actually had been weighed in the same balance as he was weighing Job, what would be his fate? If God were to really function according to Bildad's narrow concept of justice, what would happen to him?

The hypocrisy produced by judgmental assumptions doesn't lead a person surrounded by mystery to clarity. It only increases the fog of confusion. It frustrates; it antagonizes; it alienates.

Grace is the antidote to judgment and hypocrisy. Grace does not assume. It is the pathway for empathetic listening. It is the essence of the gift of two ears and an open heart to the wandering traveler.

HOLDING FAST TO DOGMATIC RHETORIC

We have become all too familiar with public discourse that seems to be driven by talking points. Politicians and political junkies have made it a fine (or not so fine) art to formulate phrases that everyone in their camp are supposed to repeat as a standard answer to any questions that might legitimately challenge their philosophic or ideological conclusions about an issue.

Much of the American electorate has become frustrated with a political process that is marked not by honest give and take to solve problems but by manipulative rhetoric intended to force agendas. The "my way or the highway" attitude of opposing sides on a particular issue is seen in the political interviews on CNN, MSNBC, and Fox News. Each side digs in their heels, and no matter what, they stick to their talking points.

Questions are dodged, ducked, and brushed aside with canned answers that have little or nothing to do with the question. A "don't confuse me with the facts" political culture emboldens the talking heads to hold fast to their rehearsed bullet points. Few of them are really listening to each other because they are trying to work in their talking point once more before the host has to interrupt and say, "We're out of time and will have to leave it at that." Viewers sit there watching with disbelief and grow even more jaded.

The one trying to find their way in the mystery is no more aided in their journey by the dogmatic rhetoric of the graceless legalist than the deliberative process of government is facilitated by the talking points of a stubborn politician. The only thing to result is frustration for the one supposedly being helped.

Job was trying to find his way in the mystery. The darkness of the valley through which he traveled was increased rather than decreased by his friends' counsel. He was put increasingly on the defensive as their so called advice grew more pointed and more like a personal attack.

Job strongly challenged the presuppositions of his three friends in chapters 23 and 24, and then put the burden of proof upon them. He closed his challenge with a direct question that called them out to prove specifically their conclusions about him.

"If this is not so, who can prove me false and reduce my words to nothing?" (Job 24:25)

Bildad had staked out a position regarding Job and his suffering. His talking point was justice. He would not be moved; his heels were dug in holding fast to dogmatic rhetoric. He betrays his real motivations in chapter 25. He completely brushed Job's question aside like a politician pinned down with a question he or she doesn't want to answer.

The words of Bildad make for a great sound bite—"Dominion and awe belong to God; he establishes order in the heights of heaven." (Job 25:2)—but they had nothing to do with Job's question. They were spin intended to keep the focus off the flaws in his theological framework that he didn't know what to do with.

Job sat there in disbelief at what he just heard. I can only imagine what was going through his mind as he prepared to reply in chapter 26: "Was Bildad even listening to me? Does Bildad care at all about me? Or is it just about Bildad forcing his agenda down my throat?" The biting sarcasm of Job's response shows that he was jaded by the party line foisted upon him by Bildad.

> "How you have helped the powerless! How you have saved the arm that is feeble! What advice you have offered to one without wisdom! And what great insight you have displayed! Who has helped you utter these words? And whose spirit spoke from your mouth?" (Job 26:2-4)

The sarcastic implication was that Bildad could hold fast to his dogmatic rhetoric all he wanted but it was devoid of the Spirit of God making it worthless to the realities Job faced. The demands of Bildad's legalistic orientation didn't give life; they brought death. As 2 Corinthians 3:6 puts it, "The letter kills, but the Spirit gives life."

If there is ever a time that life giving words prompted by the Holy Spirit are needed, it is when we are in the shadows of mystery. A shadow is cast when our bodies fail us, when a loved one dies, when a crisis strikes, when the pressures of life just overwhelm us. The graceless legalist offers lifeless dogma, but grace-givers speak life through the Spirit.

The difference between life giving words and dogmatic rhetoric is like contrasting a color photograph with a black and white photograph of the same field of flowers. No doubt there are times when black and white photography has its own beauty and mystery, but when the idea is to capture the vibrancy of a field of flowers, the starkness of black and white won't do. It doesn't capture the majestic purples, the brilliant reds, the vivid yellows, and the gentle pinks.

Legalism strips the color from theology and its practical application to real life. It makes everything stark and lifeless. It removes the hues that give life its texture and depth.

In the mystery, we need someone to point our eyes in the direction of the reds and yellows, the purples and pinks, because in the darkness of a valley, the color of life is hard to see.

◊ ◊ ◊

My father gave me wise and helpful counsel when I was early in ministry and dealing with a particularly difficult interpersonal situation: "If you are going err, err on the side of grace." Many of us are familiar with this proverb, but do we apply its wisdom?

Like Bildad, the lawyers in the church today choose to err on the side of justice and its attending strict application of rules and regulations. They put people going through the mystery of life's trials, difficulties, and uncertainties in a straight jacket that only serves to further frustrate their situation.

There are others, though, who do choose consistently to err on the side of grace. They give people the room to struggle and grow. They speak life giving words of the Spirit into the mystery. They provide a touch of color to the starkness of a dark valley.

Grace-givers are gifts to you and me. Like the wonderful, unassuming people who have a story to share to help us sort out our story, let us embrace the grace-givers and learn from them. Then we can become ministers of grace to those who need it most.

Chapter 6

MORALISM'S
SANCTIMONIOUS ANSWERS

Segments of American Christianity, particularly within evangelicalism, have been tenaciously battling in a culture war over the last 30 years or so. Lobbying, advertising campaigns, protest marches, legislative and ballot initiatives, and electoral organizing have been employed in the battle. Books have been written. Conferences and rallies have been held. Tremendous energies and resources have been invested in the fight.

What has been the objective of the evangelical right's culture war? To advance an agenda of morality in American life and politics. In general, who could argue with that? But when we get behind the surface of the culture warriors' agenda, there are some real problems.

First, morality is defined exclusively on their terms, and aside from the abortion issue, it is largely defined along the lines of sexuality. This moral agenda is fairly limited in scope. In the attempts to advance morality within the culture, sometimes tactics that are at best questionable and at worst downright immoral themselves—gossip and slander, misrepresentation, distortion, manipulation, etc.—are used in service to the cause.

Second, moral behavior without Jesus may have some societal benefits, but it doesn't get anyone closer to God. Abstinence until marriage without Jesus doesn't get a person closer to God. Heterosexuality without Jesus doesn't make a person closer to God. Adoption instead of abortion without Jesus doesn't make a person closer to God.

Third, Jesus didn't call the church to conquer the world with a moral agenda, but to lovingly point the way to God. There is an obvious note of condemnation in much of the tone, language, and tactics of the culture warriors. Not only has the evangelical right failed to pass laws to enforce its favored moral behaviors, it has alienated the larger culture to a significant degree and undermined its own spiritual influence.

Other problems also exist with the evangelical right's culture war, but the purpose of referencing its moral agenda here is not to provide a comprehensive treatment of the movement. It is simply to demonstrate in a general sense that moralism is an insufficient philosophical basis for how we approach life.

This is the point of Colossians 2:21-23: "'Do not handle! Do not taste! Do not touch!'? These are destined to perish with use, because they are based on human commands and teachings. Such regulations indeed have an appearance of wisdom, with their self-imposed worship, their false humility, and their harsh treatment of the body, but *they lack any value in restraining sensual indulgence.*" (emphasis mine) The answer to the shortcomings and sins, challenges, and mysteries of life is not a stepped up effort at pious activity.

This should not be understood as antagonistic to holiness. In fact, it upholds a correct view of holiness. Piety is not holiness. Moral behavior or refraining from immoral behavior is not holiness. True holiness is not self-attained. It is not the product of doing or not doing certain things. Holiness is not something we do; it is what we are.

Job's third friend, Zophar, was a moralist. He would have fit right into the front lines of today's cultural warriors. Zophar is the most emotional of the three who tried to provide answers for the mystery in which Job found himself. He comes from the viewpoint of piety. He gives great attention to moral actions. To him, morality held back the hand of God's judgment and wrath; therefore, anyone who came up short of what he considered to be moral simply would not be tolerated.

BEING OVERLY CONCERNED WITH ROOTING OUT SIN

Name just about any well-known public figure and unflattering pictures of them have lined the checkout aisle at your local grocery store at one time or another. Tabloid journalism earns its keep by digging up dirt on the rich and famous. Its sole purpose is to uncover the sins of its latest targets and hold them up for public humiliation.

Somehow we feel a little better about ourselves when we see the broken worlds of celebrities. It gives us an easy target at which to point our finger and make our sanctimonious speeches. But in the midst of caring so much about a celebrity's indiscretions, do we or the tabloids care at all about them as a person?

This is right where Zophar lived—so interested in finding sin in the other, he couldn't see the person who was in desperate need of love and care.

"Oh, how I wish that God would speak, that he would open his lips against you and disclose to you the secrets of wisdom, for true wisdom has two sides. Know this: God has even forgotten some of your sin." (Job 11:5-6)

The one overly concerned with rooting out sin stands there pointing a condemning finger. This finger does not carry a touch of healing. It is unmoved by the plight mystery has brought upon the subject of its condemnation. It cares about piety more than the person it demands be pious. This finger pokes the disoriented traveler in the eye. It claws at the open wound on the sufferer's soul.

Job deeply felt the soul injuring impact of Zophar's wagging, shaming finger.

"I have become a laughingstock to my friends, though I called upon God and he answered—a mere laughingstock, though righteous and blameless! Men at ease have contempt for misfortune as the fate of those whose feet are slipping." (Job 12:4-5)

Zophar and Job's other two friends hadn't taken time to really listen to Job. They didn't sympathize with him. Their approach was the antithesis of St. Francis' prayer, "...grant that I may not so much seek to be understood, as to understand."

We hear a frustrated soul in the pained reply of Job to the heap of accusation.

"I desire to speak to the Almighty and to argue my case with God. You, however, smear me with lies; you are worthless physicians, all of you! If only you would be altogether silent! For you, that would be wisdom. Hear now my argument; listen to the plea of my lips." (Job 13:3-6)

Job's voice rings down through the ages to the crusaders for piety in our own day. It challenges the sanctimonious about how it is far too easy to point fingers, especially when you don't understand what it is to be in the other's shoes. If we stood where another stands, how would we feel with an extended finger pointing our way?

An encounter Jesus had with religious leaders and a woman that had been caught in adultery powerfully demonstrates the hypocrisy of moralism's long, boney finger.

> ...The teachers of the law and the Pharisees brought in a woman caught in adultery. They made her stand before the group and said to Jesus, "Teacher, this woman was caught in the act of adultery. In the Law, Moses commanded us to stone such women. Now what do you say?" They were using this question as a trap, in order to have a basis for accusing him. (John 8:3-6)

The moral arrogance and sense of spiritual superiority of the religious leaders was in overdrive. They saw an opportunity to tear down not just one person, but two. A chance to point a finger of condemnation at Jesus was an added bonus for them as they stared at this humiliated, frightened woman.

These who had become specialists at rooting out sin in others, real or perceived, had their own issues. They could dig up dirt on people with the best of them, but seemed to be oblivious to the crud in their own lives. Their holier than thou attitude was about to get a rude awakening.

> But Jesus bent down and started to write on the ground with his finger. When they kept on questioning him, he straightened up and said to them, "If any one of you is

without sin, let him be the first to throw a stone at her." Again
he stooped down and wrote on the ground. (John 8:6-8)

Many have surmised about what Jesus had written in the dirt
that day. Perhaps the words etched into the soil were instru-
mental to what happened next. We can only guess. But what we
can positively observe about this gesture has to do with the
contrast of attitudinal posture in Jesus versus the religious
leaders.

Jesus stooped; the religious leaders stood. Jesus put his finger
in the dirt; the religious leaders pointed their fingers at the
woman. Jesus reflected humility and compassion; the religious
leaders reflected pride and callousness.

The religious leaders' sanctimonious moralism had blinded
them to the three fingers on their own hand pointing back at
themselves. It also blinded them to the needs of the woman who
stood before them as little more than an object in their eyes.

Jesus gave some time for His probing question to disarm the
accusers. When their focus was directed on the sins of the other,
it wasn't hard to pick up stones. But now they had to come face
to face with their own sinful reality, and one by one the stones
dropped from their hands.

> At this, those who heard began to go away one at a time,
> the older ones first, until only Jesus was left, with the woman
> still standing there. (John 8:9)

It turns out that the sanctimonious are not as pure as they put
on. Their pointing finger serves only to hide the depth of sin and
darkness in their own souls. The moralist cannot even pass their
own test of piety. Such was true for the religious leaders of Jesus'
day. Such was true for Zophar as Job's own version of Jesus'

probing question reveals: "Would it turn out well if he examined you? Could you deceive him as you might deceive men?" (Job 13:9) The same is also true for us today. Our pointing finger serves only to condemn ourselves.

Moralism is not the solution to our sin problem; atonement is. Moralism provides condemnation; atonement provides forgiveness. Moralism leaves us hopeless to ever measure up; atonement gives us hope.

Job clung to the hope of atonement in the face of Zophar's pointing finger.

> "Who can bring what is pure from the impure? No one! ...You will call and I will answer you; you will long for the creature your hands have made. Surely then you will count my steps but not keep track of my sin. My offenses will be sealed up in a bag; you will cover over my sin."
> (Job 14:4,15-17)

Job understood what Zophar didn't; he knew what the adulterous woman of John 8 came to know: "Blessed is he whose transgressions are forgiven, whose sins are covered. Blessed is the man whose sins the Lord does not count against him." (Psalm 32:1-2)

Imagine the power in that moment when Jesus stood up and turned His attention to the adulterous woman.

> "Woman, where are they? Has no one condemned you?"
> "No one, sir," she said.
> "Then neither do I condemn you," Jesus declared. "Go now and leave your life of sin." (John 8:10-11)

How free, how loved, how valued she must have felt. All of that condemnation was now turned to forgiveness. Who brought her into all of that? The one who actually met the condition of the question, "If any of you is without sin, let him be the first to throw a stone at her." The only one who rightly could throw a stone at her was one who had no sin. Only one met that condition—Jesus. Yet He diffused the stone throwing and showered this woman not with accusation and condemnation but with love, forgiveness, and acceptance. It most certainly must have changed her world forever.

GETTING SELF-RIGHTEOUSLY INDIGNANT

My mom has always loved to play practical jokes. I'm not as big a practical joker as her, but I must have inherited some of her sense of humor. Every so often a wave of something comes over me, and I just feel compelled to pull one off.

Practical jokes can be a lot of fun, but they also carry with them certain inherent risks, namely somebody may not find the practical joke to be very funny. I've had a couple backfire on me, including one that my brother and I played on my mom when we were teenagers. We set things up to look like I had badly cut my hand. Apparently, it was pretty realistic, because my mom became so upset over one of her kids being seriously injured that she began to hyperventilate. Okay. That practical joke wasn't too funny.

There was another time growing up that one of my practical jokes backfired, this time in a more public manner. I can't tell you to this day what possessed me to come up with the thought of what I did. (Those who were not too happy about it would have, at the time perhaps, offered the suggestion of a demonic source possessing me.) But for some unknown reason, I thought it would be funny to switch the signs on the men's and women's restrooms at our church.

Let's just say that a few people in the church didn't find any humor in it at all. There was a fair amount of indignation over the pastor's kid switching the restroom signs. It was clear to me that at least one or two people not only didn't find it funny but were angry at me for doing such a thing. I thought, "What's the big deal?" but for them it was a big deal, a very big deal.

Fortunately, most people seemed to take it in stride and were not overly bothered by it. At least they didn't let on to it if they were bothered. Who knows; maybe they even went home and had a laugh about it. And graciously, my parents didn't discipline me. Knowing my mom's love for a good practical joke, she probably had a good laugh about it in private.

I wasn't emotionally scarred for life by that little episode, but I did learn a little something about what I would call the "Why, I never" dynamic. This dynamic can be triggered in us when someone does something that we would never think of doing — like switching restroom signs. Very often self-righteous indignation comes out in connection with our pet peeves.

One of my pet peeves is when people let their shopping carts in the middle of the parking lot. It especially bothers me when I come out of a store to find a cart right next to my car. My sense of indignation intensifies if the cart return is nearby. I've been known to spew nasty comments to my wife about how lazy and inconsiderate the person is who left the cart. In the name of concern for people simply doing the right thing, my heart can end up reflecting some pretty dark stuff.

Think about one of your pet peeves. What are the feelings, attitudes, thoughts, and words that come from your heart when that pet peeve is violated, when that thing you would never do is done by someone else? If we are honest with ourselves, we can get quite self-righteously indignant.

Job's refusal to admit guilt of some hidden sin for which he was suffering triggered Zophar's moralistic pet peeve. The "Why, I never" dynamic kicked in as he responded a second time to Job's attempt to make sense of the mystery.

> "My troubled thoughts prompt me to answer because I am greatly disturbed. I hear a rebuke that dishonors me, and my understanding inspires me to reply." (Job 20:2-3)

Zophar was convinced of his own righteousness and of Job's unrighteousness. To have suggested otherwise, as Job had done, would only serve to spark his ire. Zophar didn't feel the pain of those who didn't meet his moral prescriptions; he was angry at them. His self-righteous indignation was feeding on that anger.

While Bildad thought Job was getting what he deserved, Zophar thought he was getting less than he deserved, and it made him mad. Zophar had the most cutting words for Job. Eliphaz was dispassionate in his logic; Bildad harsh in his judgment. But Zophar was downright mean, and all in the name of being concerned for moral purity.

Today's moralists are often not much different. They, too, can be angry and mean. Their indignation only adds confusion to those struggling to live in the mystery. Their anger doesn't lead themselves or those they purport to try to be helping toward a deeper experience of God.

> Man's anger does not bring about the righteous life that God desires. (James 1:20)

Get rid of all bitterness, rage and anger, brawling and slander, along with every form of malice. Be kind and compassionate to one another, forgiving each other, just as in Christ God forgave you. (Ephesians 4:31-32)

It is very telling when someone advocating the need for moral purity in another does so by venting their anger.

TELLING IT LIKE IT IS

Earlier I wrote about the adventures of teaching my children to drive. There are lessons about making turns, maintaining safe following distance, checking mirrors and your blind spot before changing lanes, and dozens of other mechanics of driving a car. But there were other important things that Paul and Adrean needed to learn about being a responsible driver that had nothing to do with the act of driving the car.

We spent time talking about how to properly take care of a car. It was drilled into their heads that one of the most important maintenance items is to regularly change the oil. I showed them how to change a tire and talked with them about keeping their car clean outside and inside.

Among the various things we talked about regarding car maintenance is the way the engine cooling system works. Part of that discussion involved showing them how to remove the radiator cap. There is also a very important safety warning that I emphatically conveyed to them about taking off a radiator cap. They could receive a serious burn from engine coolant by taking off the radiator cap while the engine is still hot.

Pressure builds up in the cooling system as an engine heats up. If the radiator cap is removed before the engine sufficiently cools and the pressure subsides, the pressure in the system will forcefully escape when the seal is broken as the cap is twisted off. This results in spraying out antifreeze/coolant hot enough to sustain third degree burns. Of particular danger is being sprayed in the face and losing eyesight.

Zophar and other moralists are like a hot radiator. They get heated up by the real or perceived moral failings of others. The angry pressure of their moral outrage builds. Dealing with them is like taking off the radiator cap. They spray their pious ranting all over you, and you get burned.

Moralists pride themselves on telling it like it is. And they don't care if it hurts. They're ready for a verbal fight. Any perceived fault will not go unaddressed by them.

Zophar initially jumped into the dialogue with Job because he was offended over Job's frankness with God (Job 10:2-22). His sanctimonious indignation sprayed out and onto Job with a verbal slap in the face.

> "Are all these words to go unanswered? Is this talker to be vindicated? Will your idle talk reduce men to silence? Will no one rebuke you when you mock?" (Job 11:2-3)

Rather than demonstrating spiritual depth as Zophar thought he was doing, he showed a remarkable level of spiritual immaturity and intolerance for any view other than his own. He is a forbearer of those to this day who are quick to speak about the morality of another. "To a Zophar every man is blind who does not see as he sees, and every word offensive that bids him take pause. ...He is an example of the bigot in the presence of genius, a little uncomfortable, a good deal offended, very sure that he knows the mind of God, and very determined to have the last word."[5]

The moralist has to have the last word. In their eyes, others must answer to their idea of what is moral and righteous, or be cursed. Their views are not open for discussion. They wish not to have a dialogue but to speak a monologue. Proverbs 18:2 says, "A fool finds no pleasure in understanding but delights in airing his own opinions." Sanctimonious moralists play the part of the fool who knows how to emotionally spout off at people about how they should live and about what they should do and shouldn't do, but knows little of how to listen and learn.

Job would not capitulate to Zophar's moralistic demands. Zophar's condemning rant certainly further discomforted Job in his suffering and added frustration in the mystery, but Job also knew to whom he answered. It was not to Zophar, but to God.

"Bear with me while I speak, and after I have spoken, mock on. Is my complaint directed to man?" (Job 21:3-4)

Zophar could not and would not offer Job hope through moralism. His piety looked down its nose upon Job and caused him still deeper grief. Though Job's own suffering and the prosperity of some who truly were wicked (Job 21:7-26) didn't add up when subjected to a moralistic formula, somewhere in the mystery God would and could be found.

◊ ◊ ◊

There is a saying that goes, "Those who live in glass houses shouldn't throw stones." The reality is that we all live in glass houses. Like Zophar, today's moral crusaders pretend that they don't live in a glass house, or they are ignorant to the fact that they do. Thus, there is no hesitation to throw stones.

However, there are others like the apostle Paul who see themselves as wretched men and women that have been rescued through Jesus Christ (Romans 7:24-25) and know it is only by the grace of God that they are what they are (1 Corinthians 15:10). They know they don't have it all together and don't jump all over others who appear to not have it together either.

They don't pretend at piety, but are genuine with regard to their faith and their failures. They accept people for who they are and where they are in their journey. They are gifts to us as we struggle with our issues.

May we embrace these authentic people and learn from their example. May we, like them, come alongside of those in trouble and walk with them as fellow strugglers.

Chapter 7

THE DISTORTING INFLUENCE OF SELF-PITY

The scene is played out more than a few times on a Friday or Saturday night. Parents of a teenager have informed their daughter that she is not going to a party hosted at the home of one of her best friends. The friend's parents will not be home, and quite a number of teenagers will be at this party. Mom and Dad have decided that this is not the best environment for their daughter.

Sally, in all of her sixteen year old wisdom, has a different assessment of the situation. First, she pulls out the "don't you trust me?" card. This doesn't seem to change her parents' position.

Then she tries another angle. "You let me go over to Sarah's other times when her parents weren't home."

Her parents explain that this is different, because this is a party involving all kinds of teenagers they don't even know. Most particularly it is a party (an unchaperoned party) that will be attended by a number of boys.

Not making any headway with her argument, Sally goes back to claiming that her parents don't trust her. Around and around it goes with Sally making no progress with her parents, except to frustrate them. Then come the words that every parent of teenagers has heard at least once, "This is so unfair!"

The line has been crossed into self-pity, and the natural downward spiral further into self-pity takes on a life of its own.

"Mom and Dad, you guys never let me do anything," Sally charges. An interesting protest in light of the argument she made in favor of letting her go to the party. (i.e. that her parents permitted her to go to Sarah's house other times when Sarah's parents weren't home) But when caught in the gravitational pull of self-pity, our view of reality gets distorted.

Sally's distorted rant continues, "You don't want me to have fun; do you?"

Instead of attending her friend's party, Sally has thrown one of her own—a pity party.

Teenagers aren't the only ones who have pity parties. If we are honest with ourselves, we adults have our fair share of getting caught up in our own pity parties too.

It can come as the result of a bad fight with our spouse or from a bad performance review at work. Perhaps we are over-taken by it when yet another thing goes wrong in the middle of a frustrating project around the house. Dealing with a season of uncertainty and confusion is also a time in which we can be made vulnerable to feeling sorry for ourselves.

The longer we are in the dark valley the more likely we are to succumb to self-pity. This is especially true if others don't under-stand us or our situation, offer useless counsel, or are sharply critical.

Such was the experience of Job. His so-called friends who had come to supposedly comfort him had actually exasperated Job's situation with their worthless answers and antidotes. They pushed him over the edge past despair. Fixated upon their antagonism, Job descended into self-pity.

Back in chapter two, we explored the issues of desperation and fixation as responses to the absence of answers for the question "Why?" It is common and understandable that intense circumstances would cause us to lapse occasionally and temporarily into despair. Getting stuck there is another matter altogether.

Fixation opens the door for self-pity to firmly establish itself in our minds and hearts. Once set into motion, self-pity produces four unhealthy outcomes upon which it further feeds itself, generating a vicious soul-robbing cycle.

DEFENSIVENESS

First, self-pity puts us into a guarded posture. We feel the need to defend and justify ourselves, particularly when we sense blame (real or perceived) directed our way or that we are not understood. Reflexively we become protective of ourselves.

This reflex action toward defensiveness is like flinching or throwing up your hands to shield yourself when someone suddenly jumps out from behind a door or pretends to throw something at you (or actually does throw something at you) without warning.

As I write this chapter, autumn has come to a conclusion and all of the leaves are now off the trees. Just a few weeks ago branches and limbs were shedding their multi-colored foliage. One of those windy days as leaves were blowing here and there, my wife and I were riding in the car. I was driving, and she was in the front passenger seat. Suddenly, a leaf was blown directly into the windshield right in front of me.

My eye caught sight of the leaf just before it hit the glass, and I immediately reacted closing my eyes and turning my head away for an instant. Fortunately, my reaction was not severe enough to endanger us with risk of an accident, but it was noticeable enough for my wife to wonder what I was doing. We both enjoyed the humor of my explanation that a leaf frightened me.

Neither the reality that I was safely behind the windshield, nor the fact that this was just a leaf flying toward me prevented me from flinching. Why did I respond the way I did?

For starters, the suddenness of an object directly in front of me didn't provide enough time for my brain to make sense of the situation before the stress of that situation engaged my adrenal and nervous systems. The powers of analysis are not available in the brief moment of surprise, so before I could think about it, my reflexes kicked in to protect my face. This largely accounts for my reaction.

There is another factor, though, that I suspect added to my reaction. Without it, I likely still would have flinched somewhat, but probably to a lesser degree. My reaction was more pronounced because of a prior bad experience with a blowing leaf.

A number of years ago I was participating in a work day at the Little League complex where I was a coach and my son played baseball. It was our fall cleanup, and leaves were coming off the trees. The day we were working happened to be very windy, and leaves were blowing all around. As I walked toward the concession stand, a leaf blew directly into my face hitting me in the eye. I felt a sharp stinging sensation and blinked several times. Immediately I noticed the sensation that something was in my eye.

I went to the bathroom to check my eye in the mirror. I didn't notice anything in my eye and went back to working. But the irritation to my eye was unbearable, and it was particularly sensitive to light. Unable to be of much help, I finally went home.

Buffy checked my eye and could find nothing. Several hours later the painful sensitivity to light and irritation was still present. We called our doctor who sent me to the hospital emergency room since it was a Saturday afternoon. Two hours later I was told that I had a scratch on my cornea.

The eye drops I was given to heal the scratch did wonders within a day or two, but I don't ever want to have to experience that again. Somewhere in the light-speed synaptic connections of my brain, the leaf flying toward my windshield this fall was associated with the scratched cornea years before and interpreted as a danger to protect myself against.

When life doesn't seem fair or doesn't make sense and other people seem to, at best, not understand or, at worst, question our spirituality, it is easy to go into a self-justifying mode. Previous bad experiences condition us to react even more defensively when the situation appears to be subjecting us to the same kind of bad experience yet again.

Job reached such a limit in his season of darkness. How could all the suffering to which he had been subjected be fair? What sense could he make of it? But worse still, he was being blamed for it all. It wasn't enough to hear once that something was wrong with his soul and that he was only reaping what he had sown. He heard eight speeches in all—each one purporting to have the answer yet none really helping him.

He had heard enough. The third round of speeches from his three friends was underway, but he wouldn't let them finish. Before Zophar could get his third turn to demoralize Job any further, Job took a stand. Feeling somewhat that God was not standing up for him against these accusations, he stood up for himself. If God wouldn't defend him, he would defend himself.

"As surely as God lives, who has denied me justice, the Almighty, who has made me taste bitterness of soul, as long as I have life within me, the breath of God in my nostrils, my lips will not speak wickedness and my tongue will utter no deceit. I will never admit you are in the right..." (Job 27:2-5)

We may know in our heads that "if God is for us, who can be against us?" (Romans 8:31) but where is the line that is reached at which we respond as Job did? Where is that place in which we justify and defend ourselves instead of allowing God to be our justifier and defender? Self-pity pushes us over that line; it settles us into that place.

In contrast to self-pity, there is the plea of the Psalmist: "Look upon my suffering and deliver me, for I have not forgotten your law. Defend my cause and redeem me; preserve my life according to your promise." (Psalm 119:153-154) Our own same kind of heart cry to God moves us away from the defensiveness of self-pity. It frees us from the downward pull of justifying ourselves. It opens the way toward the satisfaction of walking in trusting dependence upon God.

ENTITLEMENT

Self-pity makes us think things like, "I deserve better than this." We believe we are entitled to have at least some level of blessing in our lives. When a period of time passes in which blessing has not been experienced (or not noticed because it is still shrouded behind the veil of mystery), we protest.

An entitlement attitude is an unwillingness to accept discomfort or inconvenience. It mistakes a privilege as a right.

When that "right" is withheld, removed, or called into question, we feel cheated.

This is exactly what happened to Job. Though he maintained great integrity throughout the unfolding of the calamities upon him, the loss of the esteem of his peers became too much as the painful mystery dragged on. The critical barbs of Eliphaz, Bildad, and Zophar were hurtful and caused Job to put up his defenses, but it also reminded him of what he had lost.

> "How I long for the months gone by, for the days when God watched over me... Oh, for the days when I was in my prime, when God's intimate friendship blessed my house...
>
> "When I went to the gate of the city and took my seat in the public square, the young men saw me and stepped aside and the old men rose to their feet... Whoever heard me spoke well of me, and those who saw me commended me...
>
> "Men listened to me expectantly, waiting in silence for my counsel." (Job 29:2,4,7-8,11,21)

How things had changed? No longer was Job respected and sought out for his advice. His words that once carried weight, his insights that previously were influential seemed not to matter now. The mystery that had surrounded his life and the derisive judgments of others conspired to rob Job of his privileged status.

It was particularly unnerving to be treated this way both by circumstance and by the people who should have been his comforters, because Job's history was one of being a sympathizing presence in the lives of others who were surrounded by life's mysteries.

> "Surely no one lays a hand on a broken man when he cries for help in his distress. Have I not wept for those in trouble?

Has not my soul grieved for the poor? Yet when I hoped for good, evil came; when I looked for light, then came darkness." (Job 30:24-26)

We can hear Job's protest, "I deserve better than this." We can feel the downward pull of self-pity upon his soul. It is so real to us, because it is our own story too.

I can think of so many times in my life when I complained that I hadn't received better treatment, when I whined that I hadn't been dealt a better hand with regard to a particular circumstance or situation. These are times when the distortion of self-pity via entitlement makes me ungrateful and discontented.

For several years, God had a man in my life who, unknown to this man, was a periodic check on my attitude of entitlement. I met Duane shortly after becoming the pastor of the church where he had come to be a follower of Christ just a few years earlier. By the time I was the pastor of the church, as well as Duane's pastor too, he was unable to come to church services any longer.

Duane was in the advanced stages of multiple sclerosis and largely confined to bed, so I would periodically go to his home to talk, share Scripture, pray, and maybe watch some television with him and his caregiver. What he called home wasn't much. It was a long ago obsolete, run down trailer. Duane's hospital bed was the main piece of furniture in the tiny living room.

Family members had, long before, stopped coming to see him. Duane's family was his caregiver and a friend who lived with him. He hadn't seen his siblings in years, didn't even know where his father was, and saw his daughter very little. He kept a school picture of her pinned to the curtain on the window next to his bed so he could always see her.

Duane's was not an easy life. Even swallowing as he sipped from a straw was sometimes a challenge. Yet nearly every time I arrived and asked, "How's it going today, Duane?" his reply was always the same. "Can't complain."

He told me on several occasions, "You know; I have everything I need. A place to stay. Good friends. And the angel God gave to me (referring to his caregiver)."

Driving away I would often think, "Can't complain? …You have everything you need? …And I complain about such petty things." Duane's gratitude and contentment, the refusal to have an entitlement attitude, challenged me many times to adjust my outlook and stop feeling sorry for myself.

Duane certainly struggled in the mystery at times. He had his questions and very few good answers. No doubt there were days when he profoundly sensed the darkness around him just as Job did, days when he cried out in protest too. But through Duane's last day on earth, which I had the privilege to spend with him, he refused to get stuck in self-pity. He didn't let it take over in his life thinking he deserved something more, better, or different. He chose to live in the mystery.

IRRATIONALITY

Self-pity makes us defensive and causes us to feel entitled to something better than what we are experiencing at the moment. From here the next step on our descent into feeling sorry for ourselves is entertaining irrational thoughts. Distortion has fully taken hold of us at this point.

The irrationality that results from self-pity (and then further feeds it) is perhaps most notably expressed in the feeling that everyone is against us. This clouding of perspective is made worse when the people, from whom we would expect support in the fog of mystery, add to our struggle.

Such was the challenge Job faced. His friends' rebukes left him feeling abandoned and alone to find his way through the mystery. His rebuttals to their unfair charges fell on deaf ears. The memories of better days tormented him. Nothing seemed to be going Job's way, and no one seemed to be there for him. Could it be that everyone had turned on him?

> "But now they mock me, men younger than I, whose fathers I would have disdained to put with my sheep dogs...
>
> "And now their sons mock me in song; I have become a byword among them. They detest me and keep their distance; they do not hesitate to spit in my face." (Job 30:1,9-10)

Could it be that even God turned on him?

> "I cry out to you, O God, but you do not answer; I stand up, but you merely look at me. You turn on me ruthlessly..." (Job 30:20-21)

The one who had been so faithful to God now questioned God's faithfulness to him. The one who had said, "Though he slay me, yet I will hope in him," (Job 13:15) now questioned whether it really could be that God doesn't care about him.

We should never underestimate the extent to which the distorting influence of self-pity can undo us. It has the capacity to disconnect us from logical thinking and send us off toward absurd conclusions.

This is powerfully illustrated in a scene from the movie *Friday Night Lights*, which is based on a true story chronicled in a book with the same title. James "Boobie" Miles has been a star running back on the football team at Permian High School in Odessa, Texas. Entering his senior year, top college recruiters are taking a serious look at him. But everything changes when he receives a serious knee injury. His hopes for a memorable senior season on a team vying for a state championship as well as a football scholarship are all in jeopardy.

The team doctor questions whether Boobie should continue to play out of concern over the risks of even more serious damage to his knee. Therefore, Boobie is sent to a sports doctor in nearby Midland. Incidentally, Midland's high school football team is an archrival of Permian-Odessa.

The scene of Boobie's visit to Midland Hospital for an MRI and to consult with the specialist to whom he was referred begins with his uncle driving him to the appointment. By this point Boobie has experienced quite a bit of frustration over his unrealized expectations for the season so far and is seen sitting in the front seat of the car sulking in a pool of self-pity.

After the MRI, the doctor comes into the room to examine Boobie's knee and to review the MRI results. The seriousness of the injury is explained to Boobie and his uncle, and he is told that he can't play in the upcoming rivalry game against Midland. A look of disbelief and horror comes over Boobie's already somber face.

Defiantly Boobie questions, "What do you mean I can't play? I'm ready to play; I'm gonna play."

The doctor attempts to help him understand the gravity of the situation with his knee and explains, "I want what's best for you."

Incensed, Boobie fires back, "How you gonna want what's best for me; you're from Midland."

Neither the doctor nor Boobie's uncle are able to dissuade him from believing that there is a fix in for him. "Who's paying you?" he accuses; "You're trying to take my football career."

Boobie had lost all perspective. He reached the point of being irrational. He was unable to see that in fact the doctor wasn't trying to hurt him, but rather help him. Self-pity had blinded him to reality and plunged him into the unreality of believing that there was some form of organized plot set against him.

Like James "Boobie" Miles, our unmet expectations and fading hopes and dreams can leave us sulking in a pool of self-pity, making us susceptible to absurd conclusions about the way things really are. One of those, as happened with Job, is the conclusion that just maybe God isn't there in the middle of the mystery, that He is off at a distance half-interestedly observing my struggle.

Certainly there are times in the mystery when people will fail us and perhaps even turn on us. Somehow in the middle of that darkness, though, your soul and mine has to hold on to the reality that "though my father and mother forsake me, the Lord will receive me." (Psalm 27:10) Even though no one else may join us there, God is in the mystery.

SELF-CENTEREDNESS

Each of the first three outcomes of and further fuel for self-pity reflect self-centeredness to one degree or another. But there is a level of self-absorption that is utterly self-centered. When we reach this point in our descent into self-pity, we do not simply reflect self-centeredness to one degree or another; we become the center.

The depth of self-pity is more than simply feeling badly about our situation and wishing for something better. It is a fundamental orientation in which everything, even the actions of God, are organized in our hearts around ourselves and what we think is best for us at the moment.

It is not unlike the proverbial child in the checkout line at the grocery store. As an adult, I revolt against such a characterization of my truly self-centered moments. I don't see myself that way. Yet, though I'm living in the frame of a man and am free from that child's seat at the front of the shopping cart, the same primal impulse that embarrassingly insisted that my mother buy me candy is at work in me today.

Most all of us have witnessed that grueling checkout scene. Many of us have been players not only as the unhappy child but also as the frustrated parent. It is a scene in which everyone is miserable.

The child insists that she must have candy. The parent, desperately hoping the clerk will speed things up, tries to direct the child's attention away from the strategically placed racks of sweets to something else.

The child is undeterred by mom's attempts at diversion. Mom pleads with her to stop.

The little girl pleads back. Mom stands firm, "I said, 'NO'!"

The moment of truth has arrived. Will the child submit herself and her desires to the will of her parent? Or will she insist that the parent act in accordance with her will?

It is interesting to notice what happens with children in those situations. One tactic employed in an effort to get the parent to capitulate is to bargain. The child pleads her case and seeks to make a deal with the one perceived to be holding out on her. The whole presentation is really all about her.

More serious matters were involved for Job than a candy bar and a parent who wouldn't buy it for him. Nonetheless, he employed a similar tactic in an effort to force the hand of God to do something about his situation. Job was placed firmly at the center with God as an onlooker orbiting around Job's self-interests.

Job begins the final portion of his long, self-pitying discourse declaring, "Does he not see my ways and count my every step?" (Job 31:4) This is not so much a celebration of God's omnipresence as it is a subtle accusation that the ever-present God has refused to stand up for him against his friends' charges. Job had moved past defensiveness, entitlement, and irrationality to demand that God do something now.

He wraps up by throwing down the gauntlet:

"Oh, that I had someone to hear me! I sign now my defense—let the Almighty answer me; let my accuser put his indictment in writing." (Job 31:35)

It is as if Job is telling God, "Finish me off or restore me, but do something."

One will be so irreverently bold with God for only two reasons—he does not hold a very high view of God (if one at all) or he has momentarily slid God to the periphery and self to the center. Job had done the latter.

Between the backhanded compliment in verse 4 and the ultimatum of verse 35, chapter 31 is laced with "if I" or some derivative thereof. Seventeen times Job centered on himself in this bargaining session intended to make God finally capitulate. He had reached the point in which he didn't simply reflect some degree of self-centeredness; he had become the center.

Positioned at the center, when we have made it all about us, we act like God is there to serve us. The distorting influence of self-pity reverses things like looking at your reflection in the concave curve of a spoon.

> "You turn things upside down, as if the potter were thought to be like the clay! Shall what is formed say to him who formed it, 'He did not make me?' Can the pot say of the potter, 'He knows nothing?'"
> ...Yet, O Lord, you are our Father. We are the clay, you are the potter; we are all the work of your hand.
> (Isaiah 29:16; 64:8)

The message of Isaiah describes what happened to Job at his darkest hour in the depths of self-pity. It is a message that describes our own self-pitying, self-centeredness, and need of confession and repentance.

◊ ◊ ◊

Eighteenth century German hymn writer and minister Gerhart Tersteegen wrote: "As long as we want to be different from what God wants us to be at the time, we are only torment-ing ourselves to no purpose."[6] Self-pity is the act of tormenting ourselves to no purpose.

When did a pity party ever make someone feel better? It only makes a person feel worse.

Pity parties aren't fun. There's no music to dance to. The food is bitter. The punch bowl is empty. And our only friends at the party are a set of pouting triplets—me, myself, and I.

Stay away from the pity parties. Instead throw a party fit for a king—one that is filled with worship, thanksgiving, and praise to God. Dance to the music of heaven, even when its tune is unfamiliar.

Chapter 8

Getting Our Theology in Balance

I have wondered why a grandfather clock is called that. In the case of the one that sits in our home, the name makes sense. It was a clock that was my grandfather's until he and my grandmother gave it to Buffy and me as a wedding gift. What's more is the fact that my grandfather built the cabinet and assembled the clock works into the cabinet.

Initially, the clock had been a gift from my grandfather to my grandmother. Then, he made one for each of his four children, including my mother. After that, my grandfather made another clock for himself and my grandmother. That's when they gifted his first clock to me, his oldest grandchild.

That clock has been with Buffy and me for 25 years and has moved with us each of the times we have taken up a new residence. It stood in the foyer of our previous home where it faithfully chimed off the hours and quarter hours until one day when I discovered that it had mysteriously stopped.

For a while, our grandfather clock only displayed the correct time twice a day. Its hands had been permanently fixed at 9:13 for many weeks. The day it stopped running, I tried to restart it.

As I moved the pendulum to the one side of the cabinet to release it and restart the perpetual swing that keeps the clock running, it over-swung in the opposite direction banging into the other side of the cabinet.

Years of experience and several moves with this clock told me what was wrong. Either the cabinet or the rocker arm for the pendulum had gotten out of balance. I didn't have the time that day to make whatever adjustments would be needed to correct the problem and permit the clock to keep running. I simply stopped the pendulum and planned to deal with it later.

The imbalance of the clock causes the pendulum to over-swing in one direction and under-swing in the other direction. Momentum is lost each time the pendulum moves to the under-swing side. It doesn't swing as far back to the over-swing side. The cumulative effect over dozens of swings is a pendulum that stops moving and is dead still resulting in a clock that only has the correct time twice a day.

Something similar can happen with our theology, particularly in its practical outworking in our lives, if we are not intentional about staying in balance. It has been said that a fanatic is someone who won't change their mind and won't change the subject. Such a person is someone out of balance. One idea, principle, or belief takes precedence over all others to the point of unhealthy extremes.

Lopsided theology loses practical momentum in the realities of life, particularly in the mystery. It may be technically correct occasionally (like my clock that had the correct time twice a day), but it really doesn't work.

This is what happened with Job's friends and ultimately with Job in his reactive responses to them. Three rounds of theological debate over the course of twenty-eight chapters (Job 4-31) filled with imbalanced assertions about God, Job, and the meaning of suffering left them all at a dead end.

A fourth friend who had been listening to all of this finally stepped into the discussion to bring about some much needed balance.

> So these three men stopped answering Job, because he was righteous in his own eyes. But Elihu son of Barakel the Buzite, of the family of Ram, became very angry with Job for justifying himself rather than God. He was also angry with the three friends, because they had found no way to refute Job, and yet had condemned him. Now Elihu had waited before speaking to Job because they were older than he. But when he saw that the three men had nothing more to say, his anger was aroused. (Job 32:1-5)

Elihu's impassioned plea that would follow was prophetic in nature and accomplished three things—pointed out the inconsistencies of their theological posturing; was the comforting help to Job the other three friends weren't; and prepared the way for the Lord to speak directly to Job. The things he said came closest to the truth, because he took a more balanced approach.

Elihu's voice echoes through the ages and speaks to us today. It moves us away from theological debate to theological consideration. It leads us away from the extremes that cause division instead of unity and which tear down rather than build up.

His voice calls us away from our narrow, dogmatic, self-justifying theologies that rob mystery of its beauty and power. He speaks into our lives about getting our theology in balance, which will lead us closer to the heart of God, closer to where the truth is really found.

DYNAMIC TENSION

It is important to note that theological balance should not be understood in terms of simply finding the most centrally located compromise between competing ideas. It is also not attempting to simply find where there are places of agreement upon which to stand.

Theological balance is less about what happens at the middle ground and more about what happens at the respective edges. What's involved here is the counterintuitive reality of dynamic tension.

Theological balance does not happen when we run to the center and stay there. That is like the moment when I reached into the clock cabinet and stopped the pendulum. The pendulum was perfectly centered, but the clock wasn't running.

The proper functioning of the clock requires something other than a perfectly centered pendulum. Movement is required to generate the tick. The continued movement of the pendulum, which generates a continued tick and a clock that keeps time more than twice a day, depends upon what happens at the edges.

My grandfather taught me how to determine if the swing of the pendulum was just right to keep it going. He told me to hold the bob of the pendulum so that it just barely touches the side of the clock cabinet. Then he said to keep my eye on the opposite side of the clock cabinet as I release the pendulum. I need to watch to see if the bob of the pendulum comes almost in contact with that side of the cabinet.

If it bangs against the cabinet, things are out of balance to that side. If it comes up short by more than a tiny space, things are out of balance to the other side. In both cases, the pendulum will eventually stop. The solution is not found in the center, it is at the edges. One side or the other of the clock needs to be heightened or lowered.

Dynamic tension may be better understood by thinking of a piece of string being held at either end. The only way for the string to be taut is to pull at both ends in opposing directions. You simply cannot make the string taut by holding on to the middle of it. In fact, the opposite happens.

Theological balance is not static. Like the pendulum, there is movement. Like the taut string, it is pulled from both sides. We move back and forth between apparently opposing ideas. Each expresses a truth, but alone do not constitute full truth. Neither side of the theological pendulum is necessarily fully wrong; it is just incomplete without the other side.

Theological balance resists running to one side or the other; it also resists simply camping out in the center. Instead, it brings both sides into dynamic tension. It moves the pendulum back and forth evenly between one side and the other.

We struggle greatly to live in the mystery because of our penchant for "either/or" thinking. Theological balance is "both/and" thinking that allows for mystery and celebrates its wonder.

This was touched upon somewhat in chapter one as part of exploring the interplay between the sovereignty of God and our choices. Sovereignty versus free will has been a long, ongoing debate. It seems most often to be approached from the "either/or" perspective. Getting our theology in balance moves things from a debate over sovereignty versus free will to a conversation about sovereignty *and* free will.

It is like the old "nature versus nurture" arguments. Eventually, we wised up and came to realize it is not nature or nurture but rather nature *and* nurture.

Elihu had heard enough of the "either/or" thinking and spoke up to offer a different approach. His approach shows the way for us into the dynamic tension that leads to a more complete (though not perfect) understanding of God, ourselves, and the story of our lives that unfolds at times in some unexplainable ways.

HUMILITY

The recurring debate about whether to bring instant replay to baseball, as football has had for many years, was fueled again during the 2009 World Series between the New York Yankees and Philadelphia Phillies. Plays in two consecutive innings in Game 2 made clear that the umpire got it wrong, that what he saw wasn't really what happened.

The first missed call came in the bottom of the seventh inning with the Yankees leading the Phillies 3-1. Johnny Damon was hitting for the Yankees with Jorge Posada on first base. A rally could have broken the game wide open for the Yankees who lost the opener of the Series at home and didn't want to go to Philadelphia for game three trailing two games to none.

Damon hit a low line-drive to first baseman Ryan Howard, who caught the ball and threw to second for a tag out of Posada who advanced thinking Howard had trapped the ball. The umpire at first ruled Howard had caught the ball, thus forcing the second base umpire to call Posada out for the double play and squelching any rally the Yankees may have had.

The Yankees saw it differently than the first base umpire. They argued that Ryan Howard had trapped the ball, not caught it on the fly. The umpires gathered to consult with each other, which happens from time to time in baseball. I've seen a number of calls changed because such a meeting resulted in one or more of the other umpires clearly seeing the play better and differently. This time no such consensus to change the call emerged from the umpires' huddle. But the television instant replay clearly and indisputably showed they missed it. Howard had indeed trapped the ball.

A few minutes later in the top of the eighth inning the Phillies were now hitting while still trailing the Yankees 3-1. Chase Utley was at the plate with no outs and Shane Victorino on first. Utley grounded to the second baseman who proceeded to throw to Derek Jeter covering second base to turn the double play.

The throw to first base was very close with Utley hustling down the first base line. He was called out to complete the double play and end the inning. But again, instant replay showed decisively that the umpire got it wrong.

We tend to be quite harsh toward umpires who miss calls like that. However, it must be kept in mind that they see it once at full speed from only one angle. They are only human after all.

The humanness that gets in the way of umpires making the right call every time is also at work in our theological construction and application. Life unfolds around us at full speed, and we get one look at it from our limited perspective. We see things a certain way, but we could be wrong.

A great problem in so many of our theological debates is the lack of an attitude of humility. This is what had happened to Job and his three friends. Each was sure they had the answers. In each of their own minds, their perspective was the right one, and any other was wrong.

Elihu stepped into their stalemate from a different place. He challenged the lopsidedness expressed in the various speeches, yet did so with a humble spirit.

"I am just like you before God; I too have been taken from
clay. No fear of me should alarm you, nor should my hand be
heavy upon you." (Job 33:6-7)

He clearly understood his own limitations and did not set
himself up as a final arbiter of truth. He didn't come to them in
proud assurance of his theology over against theirs but rather
with a humble contribution for their consideration.

"Hear my words, you wise men; listen to me, you men of
learning. For the ear tests words as the tongue tastes food. Let
us discern for ourselves what is right; let us learn together
what is good." (Job 34:2-4)

Elihu suggested that debate be turned into conversation, that
efforts to convince be turned into readiness to learn. He recognized that no one, including himself, has a corner on the truth
and that other perspectives are needed to get us closer to the
truth.

We are all susceptible to being blind to certain aspects of the
reality of a situation. Even those who are godly suffer from these
limitations. It happened to Paul and Barnabas in their dispute
over whether to take Mark on their second missionary journey
(Acts 15:36-39).

Paul saw Mark as a hindrance to ministry. This was based on
the experience of Mark leaving them during the first missionary
journey. Paul's perspective was one focused on getting a job
done, not so much on mentoring a young man for ministry.

Barnabas brought another perspective, a needed perspective.
Barnabas, the encourager (Acts 4:36), saw the potential in Mark.
His perspective was one that focused on developing people to
get the job done.

We find later in Scripture that Paul had not been completely right about Mark. Paul himself wrote in 2 Timothy 4:11, "Get Mark and bring him with you, because he is helpful to me in my ministry." His earlier perspective of getting a job done was not necessarily a wrong one; it just lacked another perspective necessary to give him a balanced view of the potential of this young, promising man.

How often do we miss the bigger picture because we are so focused in on a particular perspective? That's not to say your perspective or mine is necessarily wrong. But are there other perspectives to which we must listen and give consideration to enlarge our view of how things really may be? This will not happen without an attitude of humility.

THE VOICE OF THE SPIRIT

Taking on an attitude of humility is an important first step toward getting our theology in balance. But it doesn't stop there. It is also critical that we listen to the voice of the Spirit of God.

When Elihu spoke up, he did so out of the prompting of the Holy Spirit.

> "I am young in years, and you are old; that is why I was fearful, not daring to tell you what I know. I thought, 'Age should speak; advanced years should teach wisdom.' But it is the spirit in a man, the breath of the Almighty, that gives him understanding. It is not only the old who are wise, not only the aged who understand what is right.
>
> "...For I am full of words, and the spirit within me compels me..." (Job 32:6-9,18)

All the wisdom and experience of age was trumped when the younger Elihu spoke, because his words were not simply human understanding but an expression of the deep things of God. These deep things are only perceived by divine assistance.

> The Spirit searches all things, even the deep things of God. For who among men knows the thoughts of a man except the man's spirit within him? In the same way no one knows the thoughts of God except the Spirit of God. We have not received the spirit of the world, but the Spirit who is from God, that we may understand what God has freely given us. This is what we speak, not in words taught us by human wisdom but in words taught by the Spirit, expressing spiritual truths in spiritual words. (1 Corinthians 2:10-13)

Sometimes we reason ourselves in a circle only to prove the depth of the mystery that surrounds us and the infinite gap between human understanding and divine wisdom. We over-think the meaning and purpose of a setback at work, an uncertainty about our future, a relationship over which we are concerned, or a series of misfortunes. We guess and second-guess. Then at the end of it all, we are as confused as before, if not more confused.

There are things too deep to understand from the human perspective. They elude our best thinking and most brilliant insights. These are matters of spiritual wisdom that can only be learned through the gracious ministry of the Holy Spirit to us.

In my early to mid-20s, my left knee began to give me trouble. Certain ways I would bend it caused me pain. The frequency and intensity of painful flexing of the knee increased into my late 20s. Eventually, I talked to a doctor about it. Ultimately, I was referred to a specialist who examined my knee and then ordered an MRI. A week or two later I had arthroscopic surgery.

An MRI produces multi-layered images of tissue, joints, and organs deep inside the body and can show things to a doctor that a routine exam wouldn't reveal. My left knee looked normal from the outside. It felt normal to the doctor's touch as he poked around the joint with his fingers.

Had I tripped on my front sidewalk and gashed my knee open on the cement, the problem would have been fairly obvious to casual observation. The cut, deep as it may be, is at the surface. The problem with my knee was not observable at the surface, other than the symptom of pain it caused. Something was going on at a deeper level. Whatever was happening in there could only be detected using an MRI. It gave the doctor eyes inside of my knee.

On the surface of much of life, theology, and the intersection of the two, things look one way but in reality are something different. The truth of the matter lies at a level too deep for us to fully grasp or understand. Much of our superficial human reasoning concludes things that are at worst incorrect and at best incomplete. We only need to listen to the assertions of Job and his three friends to see that.

We are like them. Quick to propose answers for the mystery. Ready with our theological premises. Sure about our perspective on the matter. And often off-base. Life is too complicated not to listen to the voice of the Spirit.

EMBRACE MYSTERY

Several years ago, my wife and I had just purchased a new dining set and had painted the walls in the dining room. All that was left in our dining room facelift was to change the light fixture. We searched for days trying to find one that was just right. Finally, we had our new dining room lighting.

The only thing remaining was to take down the old lighting and install the new. I had some time a few days later and got to work. The first task before me was to go to the electrical panel in the garage and turn off the breaker for the circuit on which the dining room lighting was located. I went back into the house and sure enough there was no power to the light.

I climbed the step ladder to begin the process of removing the old light fixture. As I began disconnecting the wires at the box in the ceiling, I noticed an extra set of wires running through it connected with wire nuts. The ends of the wires for the light were a little short and made working in the tight space difficult, especially with that extra set of wires running through the box.

To make a little more room to work, I decided to temporarily disconnect the ends of the extra set of wires from each other. I figured I would take off the wire nut and bend the ends back and out of the way. As I grabbed hold of the bare end of the wires, a surge of electricity shot through my fingers and up my arm.

Wow! What a shock, both literally and figuratively.

An assumption I made had proven to be quite wrong. When I saw the extra set of wires, it seemed strange that so much was running through the box that was supposed to only house the connection for the light fixture. But I had seen other things like that in our house before. I just assumed someone had cheated and used the fixture box as a junction box for another line on the same circuit.

Was I ever wrong. Why would two separate circuits run through the same box? But they did. Why wouldn't have someone labeled the box or wires to warn someone about the situation? But no one had.

The big lesson I learned from that shocking episode is not only good wisdom for electrical work, but for navigating the mysteries of God and of our lives in this world. When things don't seem to make sense, don't make assumptions.

Job's situation didn't make sense at first glance. There was no apparent explanation. But Job and his three friends couldn't stand not having a reason. "Why" couldn't remain unanswered.

The friends tried to force connecting the dots through limited theological perspectives. They made assumptions about Job and his spiritual integrity. Job, on the other hand, couldn't connect the dots. So he made assumptions about God and His justice. Wouldn't they all have been shocked had they suddenly known of what we were given a glimpse back in Job 1 and 2?

Elihu, with a touch of sarcasm, puts the assumptions of both Job and his friends to the test. Even Elihu reflects a bit of the karma-like theology of the other four that we examined in chapter three. Yet at a few places, he breaks through the assumptions that come from theological imbalance to effectively say, "Guys, none of us has this thing all figured out. We're just making assumptions about the way things are."

> "Not one of you has proved Job wrong; none of you has answered his arguments. Do not say, 'We have found wisdom; let God refute him, not man.' But Job has not marshaled his words against me, and I will not answer him with your arguments.
> "They are dismayed and have no more to say; words have failed them." (Job 32:12-15)

"But if he (God) remains silent, who can condemn him? If he hides his face, who can see him? Yet he is over man and nation alike... (Job 34:29)

"So Job opens his mouth with empty talk; without knowledge he multiplies words." (Job 35:16)

God often works in ways that don't make sense to us mortals. Our assumptions about what He must be doing can take us off in a direction leading away from His actual purposes. No less was the case for Peter when he heard the words of Jesus that didn't compute in his mind.

From that time on Jesus began to explain to his disciples that he must go to Jerusalem and suffer many things at the hands of the elders, chief priests and teachers of the law, and that he must be killed and on the third day be raised to life.
Peter took him aside and began to rebuke him. "Never, Lord!" he said. "This shall never happen to you!"
(Matthew 16:21-22)

Jesus' words seemed like crazy talk to Peter. How could any of what He was saying be true? It didn't square up with Peter's assumptions of what the Messiah was supposed to do and to be. Under the influence of his limited theological perspective, Peter missed the beauty, tragedy, and marvel of what was about to happen.

God may be working in your life right now in an unseen, unfathomable way behind the scenes of the dark veil that surrounds your situation. The apparent setback you've experienced may actually be the first step toward a new and exciting chapter to unfold in your life. Perhaps the pain that won't leave is a gracious gift not to hurt you but to lead you into a deeper experience of life, a greater compassion for others who hurt, and a fuller realization of God's sustaining power.

I can't say for sure why you are experiencing a deep valley. You may not be able to explain the dark night of your soul either. But you and I can live in the comfort that God's ways are higher than our ways and His thoughts are higher than our thoughts (Isaiah 55:8-9).

The fog of our situation can make it feel like God has turned a blind eye or a deaf ear. We pray, and the veil of mystery seems to only grow thicker. As you and others close to you struggle to find answers, you wonder why God hasn't given an answer of His own.

But could the answer be the mystery itself? Could the mystery of God's ways be the point? Instead of making assumptions when things don't make sense, embrace the mystery of God's ways.

Elihu shattered the assumption of Job that God wasn't responding to his situation by pointing him to the mystery of God.

> "But I tell you, in this you are not right, for God is greater than man. Why do you complain to him that he answers none of man's words? For God does speak—now one way, now another—though man may not perceive it." (Job 33:12-14)

The problem wasn't that God was off at a distance unconcerned with Job's plight. He wasn't silent; He was just speaking in a way other than what Job and his friends assumed He would speak. The way God had responded before was not the way He was responding this time.

God has not turned a blind eye or a deaf ear to you and me in our dark nights of the soul. He is not absent as we struggle for answers from our limited theological perspectives. He is not silent; He is not uninvolved. He is working in ways other than what we would assume. He is there in the mystery the whole time.

EXALTED VISION OF GOD

Getting our theology in balance is not so much a product of effectively systematizing a disparate collection of facts and bits of information about God and His purposes for creation. It is more about having a right posture of the heart.

Satisfied with the apparent contradictions as we live in a place of dynamic tension. Humility to accept that we don't have a corner on the truth. Recognition that there are things deeper than we understand and that require listening to the voice of the Spirit. Embracing mystery as an alternative to making assumptions about things that don't make sense. These are matters of the soul. And chief among the matters of the soul that help to get our theology in balance is how we view God.

A. W. Tozer points out:

> What comes into our minds when we think about God is the most important thing about us.
>
> The history of mankind will probably show that no people has ever risen above its religion, a man's spiritual history will positively demonstrate that no religion has ever been greater than its idea of God.[7]

And J. I. Packer simply yet profoundly observes, "Those who know God have great thoughts of God."[8]

Unfortunately, we have reduced God to neatly packaged definitions and confined Him to our carefully formulated systematic theologies. We use lofty terms in reference to His nature and character, but in practical everyday life, we may not have as large a vision of God as we claim in our creeds and doctrinal statements.

If we have any hope toward getting our theology to some reasonable place of balance that will be of actual help in real life, we must be captured by an exalted vision of God.

Elihu shifted gears in the last portion of his response to Job and his three friends. A bulk of what Elihu had to say (Job 32-35) was directed at the faulty reasoning of the four men who had been debating theological points. But his ending exclamation point (Job 36-37) directed full attention to cultivating great thoughts about God.

First, Elihu comforts Job with the thought that although God is mighty and exalted He is also tender and caring.

> "God is mighty, but does not despise men...
> "He is wooing you from the jaws of distress to a spacious place free from restriction, to the comfort of your table laden with choice food." (Job 36:5,16)

An exalted, high view of God is not one in which God is feared in the sense of trembling terror. "God is love... There is no fear in love. But perfect love drives out fear." (1 John 4:16,18) He is feared in the sense of awesome wonder. He is mighty and gentle—perfectly, infinitely, and always both.

Elihu then pointed Job's frame of reference away from the limiting perspectives of himself and his demoralizing counselors, not to a theological counterpoint but to the grandeur of God Himself. He was painting the picture for Job of an exalted vision of God.

"God is exalted in his power. Who is a teacher like him? Who has prescribed his ways for him, or said to him, 'You have done wrong'? Remember to extol his work, which men have praised in song. All mankind has seen it; men gaze on it from afar. How great is God—beyond our understanding! The number of his years is past finding out." (Job 36:22-26)

God transcends all of our theological wrangling over this or that finer point of doctrine. Our limited perspectives are shown for what they really are before His limitlessness. At the end of our best definitions of God and descriptions for why things happen in this world as they do is the incomprehensible reality of who God really is.

An exalted vision of God sees that nothing compares to Him, no one is in His league. It reminds me of the *American Idol* auditions that take place each year.

The exciting part of *American Idol* comes in the second half of the season when the best singers are competing against one another. The funny part comes in the first half of the season when potential future Grammy Award winners and tone deaf wannabes are featured back to back. The incomparability of one to the other is almost painful to watch.

One of the best examples of this was in the third season of *American Idol*. That was the year of William Hung and his infamous rendition of "She Bangs." Crazy enough, he scored a minor recording contract and made a few appearances, but it wasn't for the quality of his singing. His cult following was really about how out of tune he sang.

In stark contrast was that year's *American Idol* winner, Fantasia. Her powerful voice made beautiful music that captivated and moved those who heard it. William Hung's singing, by comparison, was just noise that made people laugh and sometimes grimace. In reality, there was no comparison. There is no comparison when it comes to God.

> For who in the skies can compare with the Lord? Who is like the Lord among the heavenly beings? In the council of the holy ones God is greatly feared; he is more awesome than all who surround him. O Lord God Almighty, who is like you? You are mighty, O Lord, and your faithfulness surrounds you. (Psalm 89:6-8)

Any of our perspectives or answers for the deepest, most complicated issues of life is just noise compared to the beauty of God and His ways. Our attempts to explain what only God can fully understand are at best laughable and at worst embarrassingly painful.

An enlarged vision and concept of God may or may not lead us to clear answers for the mystery. Most times it won't. But that's not the greatest goal for us in life anyway, though we often think and act as though it is.

The Westminster Shorter Catechism taught that the chief purpose of a human being is to glory God and enjoy Him forever. Though having answers to life's problems and challenges is not a bad thing (It's a good thing when we get them.), it is not critical to fulfilling our purpose nor to being fulfilled. However, experiencing God is.

But who are we experiencing both in the mountaintops and in the valleys, in the times of great clarity and of great mystery? Our concept of God, the nature of our vision of Him, determines the quality of that journey.

As Elihu's response came toward an end, Job was about to encounter God in a powerful way (We'll get to that in the next chapter.), and it would change his outlook and perspective. It would bring him to a new level of self-awareness and God-awareness.

Elihu prepared the way for this encounter with God. As he cast the exalted vision of God, Elihu began to paint a picture of a rainstorm.

"He draws up the drops of water, which distill as rain to the streams; the clouds pour down their moisture and abundant showers fall on mankind." (Job 36:27-28)

The word picture was perhaps prompted by an actual storm gathering on the horizon. Pointing to the darkening skies and distant lightning, Elihu helps Job see the awesome presence of God in the storm.

"God's voice thunders in marvelous ways, he does great things beyond our understanding...

"Listen to this, Job; stop and consider God's wonders. Do you know how God controls the clouds and makes his lightning flash? Do you know how the clouds hang poised, those wonders of him who is perfect in knowledge?"
(Job 37:5,14-16)

This was not just a word picture about raindrops, thunder, and lightning; it was also about the storm that had been raging in Job's life. He had been under a dark cloud for some time now. When would the sun shine on his life again? But in the darkness, there was God.

The thunderstorm that now was bearing down on them, the one being described by Elihu, became a living illustration. The drama reached a climax when Elihu finished speaking—"Then the Lord answered Job out of the storm." (Job 38:1)

It is interesting to note that God never tells Job why the things happened to him that did. His answer from the storm was not providing a solution to the puzzle that Job and his three friends couldn't solve. It was letting Job know that God was right there in the storm. If nothing else made sense, it was enough that God was there.

Is God enough for you in the absence of answers to the mysteries you encounter? Your response to that question may say a lot about what kind of vision you have of God.

Let the fullness of who God really is capture you. Let the majesty of His splendor and power, as well as the comfort of His gentleness, overtake you. Allow the incomprehensible, incomparable nature of God to captivate your imagination. Allow His presence to reach out from within the storm to touch you.

Chapter 9

ENCOUNTER WITH GOD

George signed up with an online dating service wondering what might happen and figuring he had nothing to lose. The first dating experience that resulted from his profile on the website was okay but didn't develop into a relationship.

A couple weeks passed, and then George saw Amelia's profile online. He was interested; so was she. They got to know each other a bit more online. He was still interested; so was she. A date was arranged.

George was anxious, nervous, and excited as the date with Amelia approached. His interest in her was fairly high, as were his hopes that this time things might work out. George later told me he was awestruck when the moment arrived at which he actually encountered Amelia on that first date.

Things did work out for them. I had the privilege to conduct their wedding within a year after they had first met on that hopeful, awesome evening. On a beautiful autumn afternoon, George was awestruck again as his bride came down the aisle to meet him.

Email, instant messaging, and online social networking are great tools for interacting with other people. But nothing beats a personal encounter. The wonder and beauty of relationship comes when we are up close and personal. There is something inexplicably awesome when we interact soul to soul, spirit to spirit with another.

No less is true with God. It is one thing to have an interest in God; it is quite another to meet Him. It is one thing to connect across the distance between my world and His; it is quite another to experience Him manifestly right in the middle of my story. And when we have a personal encounter with God, it leaves us awestruck.

We are not the same when we encounter God. The mystery takes on a strange beauty. We discover it is not necessarily a distance between us and God, but is a means to knowing Him more profoundly. New perspectives come into view. We freshly interpret our journey. And like Moses' face shined after talking with God (Exodus 34:29-35), our lives take on a hopeful, awesome radiance.

EXPERIENCE BEYOND EXPLANATIONS

An encounter with God leaves us awestruck by God himself. This encountering God is not something spiritually generic; He is not a force or energy of the universe. He is personal and has being. This is so much His essence that when Moses asked who he should say sent him, God referred to Himself as "I AM." (Exodus 3:14) Jesus, too, used the same language, "Before Abraham was born, I am!" (John 8:58)

Until George actually met Amelia, she was a name, a picture, and a description to him. He had interest, but not awe. It was the point at which he came into personal encounter with her being that Amelia became real to him and changed his life.

God is noticeably absent in His person and being from chapters three through thirty-seven in the book of Job. His name is evoked often all throughout the speeches of those chapters. There is a lot of God-talk found there, but not an encounter with God.

There are three main Hebrew names for God used throughout the Old Testament—Elohim, Adonia, and Yahweh (or Jehovah). Yahweh/Jehovah speaks particularly to God's personal covenant relationship with His people. It is the name that expresses personal encounter. It is the name used when God reached out of the storm to touch Job: "Then the Lord (Yahweh) answered Job out of the storm." (Job 38:1)

It is of particular note and importance that the use of Yahweh follows a particular pattern in the book of Job. It appears extensively through chapters one and two. But then this name for God is used only once in the next thirty-five chapters, despite all of the talk about God. Then the name Yahweh is reintroduced at the climactic point of Job's mysterious journey and appears extensively again throughout the rest of the book.

Job and his counselors got caught up in their pursuit of explanations, both of God and of why calamity had come upon Job. They had formulated all of their carefully crafted answers, yet missed out on experiencing God Himself.

God spoke from the storm (figuratively in Job's life and literally from the rain and thunder clouds overhead) to reveal Himself to Job, not simply in words and definitions but in experience. He reached forth from the mystery so that Job would encounter Him and be left awestruck by the essence of His person and being.

As God spoke from the storm, He pointed all around at creation to enlarge Job's vision of Him. He began with questions about the origins of the earth—questions that still confound to this day.

> "Where were you when I laid the earth's foundation? Tell me, if you understand. Who marked off its dimensions? Surely you know! Who stretched a measuring line across it? On what were its footings set, or who laid its cornerstone?"
> (Job 38:4-6)

God continued in verses 8-32 to focus on the wonder of creation. He kept framing it in the form of questions—ones that Job couldn't answer. No one can fully explain creation. How much less is it possible to explain the Creator?

Why then do we pour so much time into trying to force an answer to the mystery instead of simply encountering God Himself in that mystery? The encounter happens when we have an experience with God, not just an explanation of Him.

Derek Jeter was named the *Sports Illustrated* Sportsman of the Year a few weeks before I wrote this chapter. The New York Yankees' shortstop has been long admired in our home, especially by my son Paul.

Jeter's career began when Paul was in elementary school, and Paul grew up idolizing him. Pictures from *ESPN: The Magazine* and other sports periodicals of Jeter in action papered one of the walls in Paul's bedroom. He read an autobiography by the famous infielder. He kept up-to-date on television and online with everything having to do with Derek Jeter. Paul talked about him and imitated him.

One summer the Yankees were playing a three game series in Philadelphia, and we got tickets for all three games. Sometimes when attending Phillies games, we would go early to watch batting practice. One of the evenings of this particular series with the Yankees we decided to head down to Veterans' Stadium early. The main purpose was to get a closer look at Derek Jeter and possibly have Paul get his autograph.

Paul had heard about, read about, and thought about Derek Jeter; he had seen him from a distance on television and from the stands. But he had never met him personally. This was the goal that summer late afternoon.

As batting practice concluded, Derek Jeter began to make his way toward the seats next to the Yankees dugout. Kids, teenagers, and adults raced from their particular vantage points in the surrounding sections to get to where Jeter stood along the fence. One of them was Paul.

He moved as quickly as he could from where we were seated, weaving in and out of the rows and aisles. By the time he got down to the edge of the field, any semblance of a line had turned into a massive blob of people. Paul was getting within reach of his baseball idol when Jeter headed back to the dugout to begin loosening up his arm.

Paul is no less a fan of Derek Jeter for not having met him personally, but it sure would have been an amazing experience that in a small way would have been life-changing. Paul can explain all kinds of things to you about Derek Jeter, but he lacks the one thing that makes a huge difference—he has never met him nor does he know him personally.

It makes all the difference in the world when God is not just one whom we've heard about, read about, thought about, and seen from afar but is rather one we know in a personal way. And not in the clichéd "I have a personal relationship with God" way, but by way of actual experience of Him.

This is what happened to Job. He came to know God in a way that he never had before. After the encounter with God out of the storm, he declared, "My ears had heard of you but now my eyes have seen you." (Job 42:5) Job now had an experience with God, not just an explanation of Him.

What happened for Job is what the apostle Paul prayed would happen for the Ephesian Christians. It is a reality that is possible for us too.

> I keep asking that the God of our Lord Jesus Christ, the glorious Father, may give you the Spirit of wisdom and revelation, *so that you may know him better.* (Ephesians 1:17)

Paul is not praying for an increase of information about God. He is not interested in the Ephesians having better explanations of God. His heartbeat for them, and the promise for us, is found in the Greek word that is translated "know."

There are two words that would commonly be translated "know" or "to know." One is *gnosis.* This word means to know by way of intellect. It is knowledge of something or someone through information. The other word is *epignosis,* which means to know by way of experience. It is knowledge of something or someone through an encounter with the thing or the person known.

The word used in Ephesians 1:17 is *epignosis.* Paul's passion is that these Christians would experience God better. God's heart for us is not simply to reveal Himself to us so that we would know about Him, but that we would encounter Him.

A FRESH GLIMPSE

An encounter with God leaves us awestruck by God's presence. In addition to the overwhelming sense of His being is the reality of how close at hand He is. The God who can seem so distant in the middle of life's mysteries really is right there all the time. We are reminded of His closeness in the breakthrough of an encounter with Him.

Job felt God had abandoned Him. His self-justifying plea right before Elihu spoke up questioned, "Where are you, God?"

Job had not denied God's existence; nor did he even deny the reality of God's omnipresence. But he did wonder why God wasn't manifesting that presence in active participation in his life and on his behalf, at least as Job understood it from his perspective.

Was God off some other place in the world preoccupied with someone else's concern? Had He turned His head at some point and missed something? Was He not paying attention? Did He just not care enough?

Like Job, we know in our heads the correct answer to these kinds of questions is "no." Yet when they inevitably arise at those times when life doesn't make sense, we feel somewhere within us that the answer actually might be "yes." In effect, we come to believe that God has abandoned us, or at least He is only half interested in our situation.

God's transcendence—that He is beyond time and space— seems to further reinforce the sense of His distance from us and our issues. While God is altogether separate and other, He is anything but out of touch with our experience. He is not only transcendent; He is also immanent—involved within time and space. This explains why God is both infinite and intimate.

First, God pointed to the wonder of creation to demonstrate His transcendence, and thus the inexplicability of His being and His purposes. Then, He turned Job's attention to the way in which creation is sustained.

> "Do you know the laws of the heavens? Can you set up God's dominion over the earth?" (Job 38:33)

Continuing through the rest of chapter 38 and all of chapter 39, God focuses on the mysterious ways of various creatures and how they are sustained. Through it, God demonstrates His involvement in the details of what happens on this planet. In showing His presence in all of creation, it shows God's presence in Job's life and in his problems.

God has not overlooked or forgotten His other creatures, so we, as His most prized creation, certainly can rely on Him as our ever-present sustainer. Jesus taught this comforting truth with these words:

> "Look at the birds of the air; they do not sow or reap or store away in barns, and yet your heavenly Father feeds them. Are you not much more valuable than they?" (Matthew 6:26)

> "Are not two sparrows sold for a penny? Yet not one of them will fall to the ground apart from the will of your Father. And even the very hairs on your head are all numbered. So don't be afraid; you are worth more than many sparrows." (Matthew 10:29-31)

God brings us into an encounter of Himself through a thundering voice or a gentle whisper. And either way, we come to see that God has not abandoned us.

Job briefly spoke in the middle of his encounter with God (Job 40:3-5) simply to say that all he had concluded about God being absent from his place of pain and misery was wrong. God had been there all along; Job just lost sight of Him.

Most of us have seen little children who begin to panic when they lose sight of their mother or father. One such time that comes to mind was following a church service when a group of us were standing around talking. One of the people in our gathering was the mother of a toddler who was being held by another person participating in our conversation.

The mother was standing next to me trying to stay in view of her little one. At one point, she dropped back from the circle of people that were standing there to look through her purse or diaper bag for something. All the while she was still in sight for her daughter.

But then it happened. I moved toward another person to whom I was directly speaking and right into the line of sight between toddler and mom. It only took a few moments before the crying started.

Realizing what I had done, I quickly moved out of the way. At the same time, the mother turned directly toward her daughter so she could see her. The moment the child caught a glimpse of her mother, a look of calm and reassurance came over her.

An encounter with God gives us a fresh glimpse of Him. Though we wrestle with the question "Why?" and struggle with mystery, we see in the glimpse of God that we've not been abandoned. And that settles our soul. It brings calm and reassurance.

This fresh glimpse of an ever-present, intimately involved God was the experience of David who wrote:

Where can I go from your Spirit? Where can I flee from your presence? If I go up to the heavens, you are there; if I make my bed in the depths, you are there. If I rise on the wings of the dawn, if I settle on the far side of the sea, even there your hand will guide me, your right hand will hold me fast. (Psalm 139:7-10)

When was the last time you had a fresh glimpse of God? How long has it been since you really looked to see that indeed He is actively involved in the details of your life? He is not across the distance of time and space; He is right there, right now, in the mystery.

AWARENESS

An encounter with God leaves us awestruck by God's moral supremacy. The manifest presence of God is more than about knowing He is there. Though the sense of His presence is comforting in the dark valleys and uncertainties of life, we have not fully experienced His presence if we are not humbled before the sheer reality of who He is.

Meeting God takes us into a whole new level of awareness. Because we get a glimpse of God for who He really is and what He is really like, everything else gets seen in a new light—including ourselves.

All of us have a lack of self-awareness to some degree or another. We don't see ourselves for who we really are. Other people sometimes can help us grow in our understanding of ourselves. Sometimes circumstances may teach us a thing or two about ourselves. But more than anything, encountering God helps us see ourselves more accurately.

The downward pull of self-pity had so warped Job's awareness of himself that he didn't even realize he was calling God's justice into question.

> Then the Lord spoke to Job out of the storm:
> "Brace yourself like a man; I will question you, and you shall answer me.
> "Would you discredit my justice? Would you condemn me to justify yourself?" (Job 40:6-8)

Job was overwhelmed already by the experience of God's being and presence, "I am unworthy—how can I reply to you? I put my hand over my mouth. I spoke once, but I have no answer—twice, but I will say no more." (Job 40:4-5) But now God presses in upon Job even more to reorient Job's self-understanding, to develop Job's self-awareness.

The tour of creation upon which God had been taking Job concluded by zeroing in upon two specific beasts—the behemoth (Job 40:15-24) and the leviathan (Job 41). Much has been made about what these two beasts were. Some surmise the behemoth was a hippopotamus or an elephant and the leviathan was a crocodile. Others suggest they may have been two types of dinosaurs that had survived the Genesis flood and were subsequently extinct.

What these two beasts were exactly is not really too important. The issue is the point God was trying to make to Job and ultimately to us who read this narrative. From the description of these two animals we know they were very large and very fierce. We also know that they clearly were difficult, if not impossible, for a human being to subdue.

God was effectively saying, "Job, you are no match for these terrible beasts, but they are no match for me. So, Job, how do you measure up before me?"

Thinking about impossible matchups, I am reminded of professional wrestling that I watched growing up. When I was young, Andre the Giant was the king of professional wrestling. All challengers would be soundly beaten by Andre the Giant. Huge, muscular men were no match for him.

My two brothers and I would watch wrestling on Friday nights and on Saturday mornings. We would often have matches of our own imitating the wrestling moves we saw on television. Sometimes we would even invite our sister to join us so we could have tag team matches. The winner would always triumphantly and arrogantly (just like the wrestlers we saw on television) stand in the middle of the "ring" to assert his victory.

In the universe that was contained to the basement of our house, I could be the "king of the ring." Outside of that small world I wouldn't last a minute in the ring with The Iron Sheik or Rowdy "Roddy" Piper—men that Andre the Giant barely broke a sweat tossing around the ring like rag dolls.

How would I have felt, proudly standing at the center of the "ring" in our basement, if Andre the Giant came bursting through the door? The sense of my greatness would have immediately shrunk to nothing.

This is what happened to Job that stormy day. God burst through the door into the middle of Job's little universe that had been constructed around himself. God's moral supremacy to anything Job had to offer deconstructed that little universe. Job's vision of God grew and his self-awareness did too.

Then Job replied to the Lord:
"I know that you can do all things; no plan of yours can be thwarted. You asked, 'Who is this that obscures my counsel without knowledge? Surely I spoke of things I did not understand, things too wonderful for me to know."
(Job 40:1-3)

It is not enough just to have a right concept of God; we must also have a right concept of ourselves. Only when we encounter God do we have the opportunity to really see ourselves as we are. We are made so aware of ourselves before Him that spiritual pride, which so easily creeps in unnoticed as we struggle with mystery, is able to be seen for what it is. And more importantly, it can be dealt with.

We are brought into a place in which we don't need to have all the answers nor do we attempt to provide them. We live recognizing there are things beyond our capacity to understand or know, things that are a mystery. The mystery is embraced not as a puzzle to be solved but as a God-absorbed reality into which we lean and live and are awed.

◊ ◊ ◊

I am convinced that perhaps as much as anything which contributes to stale, apathetic, typical "Sunday go to church meeting," ho-hum Christian life and experience is a lack of truly being in awe of God.

To many, God is awesome in the casual way we use the word. It's awesome when the Yankees (my favorite baseball team) come back in the bottom of the ninth to win. It's awesome to get a great deal on a car purchase. For Dick Vital, just watching a college basketball game is "awesome baby."

Cannonballs off the diving board make awesome splashes. A filet mignon steak cooked to perfection tastes awesome. Our favorite band performs an awesome concert. The autumn leaves or spring flowers have awesome color. Air conditioning on a hot summer day feels awesome.

If God is awesome like these things are awesome, we've not encountered God up close and personal. Further, the mystery will loom too large to see Him in it.

Encountering God takes awesome to a whole new level. There should be an entirely new word for it. It doesn't simply give us a momentary good feeling like all of those other awesome things do. To encounter who God is and what He is like has no human words to fully express the impact of such a meeting.

When "why" is the furthest thing from our minds or when it is the first thing on our lips, when everything seems to be making sense or when we are struggling in the mystery, the vibrancy, depth, and dynamic of our lives ultimately comes down to having a personal encounter with God.

Chapter 10

Happily Ever After

The twists and turns in the relationship of Ross and Rachel during ten seasons of the television sitcom *Friends* were many. The way they responded to each other was predictably unpredictable. They seemed destined to be together, yet strangely destined to do every imaginable thing to frustrate themselves from being together. It was never quite clear how it would all turn out with them.

The unfolding plot of "Ross and Rachel" continued as a main sub-theme throughout the series to the final episode. Rachel had landed a dream job in Paris and was planning to move there. Ross was deeply disappointed but reticent to try to convince her to stay. Deep down Rachel was wrestling with her own emotions about the two of them. True to form though, they continued the awkward dance of their confusing relationship.

The final few minutes of the last episode had come, and it looked as if the relationship that so many fans of *Friends* had hoped would work out was going to come to a certain end. Ross had finally come to the point in which he felt he had to tell

Rachel exactly how he felt and that he didn't want her to move, but only after Rachel had already left for the airport.

Ross raced to catch up to her before she boarded the plane that may have been taking her away from him forever. After first going to the wrong airport, he finally arrived at the right airport only to see her disappear into the jetway. He and their friend Phoebe ran toward the boarding area calling out Rachel's name. Hearing their pleas for her, Rachel came back out of the jetway into the boarding area with a confused look on her face.

Ross told her that he loved her and didn't want her to go. He poured out his heart to her. Overwhelmed and not knowing what to do, Rachel, true to the form of their continued confusing dance, told him, "I can't do this now." She headed back into the jetway moments later leaving Ross heartbroken.

He returned home overcome with despair of his situation. The answering machine light was blinking, and with disinterested resignation, he hit the button to listen. Rachel's voice came from the machine increasing the forlorn look on Ross's face. She apologized for how she reacted in the airport and told Ross she loved him too.

The words gave him hope and pain. For Rachel, the words coming from her own mouth gave her pause to consider what she really wanted.

She repeated what she heard herself saying, "I love you."

She said it again with newfound certainty about how she really felt about Ross.

Rachel suddenly realized that she wanted off of the plane and began to ask the flight attendant to let her off. Ross leaned hopefully toward the answering machine hanging on every word. The flight attendant was heard in the background insisting that Rachel was not getting off of the flight.

Ross yelled at the machine, "Let her off the plane."

Rachel was continuing to make her case with the attendant when the time ran out on the message.

With frustrated hope, Ross pleaded with the quiet machine, "Did she get off the plane; did she get off the plane?"

Rachel's voice is then heard again. This time from the doorway of Ross' apartment, "I got off the plane."

Everyone loves a happy ending. In the middle of the drama of story, it seems at times that it won't really happen. But when it finally does, there is relief, joy, and a sense of resolution.

The book of Job has a happy ending, and it shows how the stories of our lives can have happy endings. Unfortunately, though, the ending of Job has been subjected to much misinterpretation and faulty expectations regarding perseverance through trials.

It is quite tempting to derive a "health, wealth, and prosperity" theology from the final scene of Job's story. However, this is neither the point of the book of Job nor of any other scripture. Interpreting scripture with scripture and looking more deeply into the drama's resolution leads us to see that the happy ending is not about material blessings.

Neither is the happy ending about getting answers to all of the questions that arose from Job's dark season of the soul. In all that God said as He spoke from the storm as well as in His rebuke and challenge to Job's three friends in the final scene of the drama, He provided no explanation for what had happened to Job. In fact, instead of resolving questions, He raises more questions for which Job and his friends have no answers.

The happy ending of mystery is about growth in depth of character and in wholeness of soul and spirit. It is about a life that is truly enriched.

FORGIVING OUR OFFENDERS

The central character in all great dramas has one or more antagonists. The antagonist in your drama may be an unfair boss, a disrespectful employee, a dishonest friend, a spouse who left or parent who abused, a harsh church leader, a critical church member, a rude neighbor... (You get the point.) Whoever it may be, he or she caused or added to your pain, confusion, frustration, or trouble.

Job contended with three offenders. The men who were supposedly his friends had been anything but friendly. They deepened the misery of his dark valley. Their conduct was not only hurtful to Job; it was offensive to God.

> After the Lord had said these things to Job, he said to Eliphaz the Temanite, "I am angry with you and your two friends, because you have not spoken of me what is right, as my servant Job has. So now take seven bulls and seven rams and go to my servant Job and sacrifice a burnt offering for yourselves. My servant Job will pray for you, and I will accept his prayer and not deal with you according to your folly. You have not spoken of me what is right, as my servant Job has."
> (Job 42:7-8)

The three friends didn't just sin against Job; they sinned against God. They spoke so proudly and assuredly (and so wrongly) about what they believed God was doing. In their arrogance and lack of mercy, they claimed things about God that were not really true. Yet, God was willing to forgive them. But was Job?

How well a particular story in our life ends depends very much upon what we do with those who have offended us during the unfolding plot. Our lives can only be deepened and enriched to the degree by which we forgive.

"You have heard that it was said, 'Love your neighbor and hate your enemy.' But I tell you: Love your enemies and pray for those who persecute you, that you may be sons of your Father in heaven." (Matthew 5:43-45)

We take on the heart of Christ when we forgive our offenders. Jesus faced antagonists—the religious leaders and His Roman executioners—that were like none other. But He still prayed, "Father, forgive them, for they do not know what they are doing." (Luke 23:34)

I remember when I was young hearing about the crucifixion and wondering why Jesus didn't come off the cross and give the Roman soldiers a taste of their own medicine. After all, that's what happened in all the good guy/bad guy television shows. The bad guys harass and cause trouble, all the while seeming to get away with it as they smile derisively. But in the end, the good guy always showed the bad guys who's boss—either beating them to a pulp or shooting them dead.

Why didn't Jesus act like heroes are supposed to act and kick some Roman butt? Because He was acting greater than a hero by forgiving them. He could have taken His vengeance upon them. There was nothing they could have done to stop Him. But He chose to stay on the cross, to continue suffering, forgiving both their sin and mine.

Job responded in a similar manner to the friends who had so offended him—praying for those who had persecuted him (Job 42:9-10). He forgave them as God had forgiven him.

Bitterness is a powerful force that will keep us from the happy ending. When we hold on to bitterness, it really is holding on to us. We can't get on to enjoy all of what God has for us, because we are trapped in a fixation upon our offender(s) and what they did (or may do again) to us.

There are some things that can only be overcome by dealing with them head on. Bitterness is one of them. Another is fear. And like fear, bitterness feeds on itself. Both need to be faced proactively and undone in our lives, or they have the capacity to dominate us in unhealthy, even destructive, ways.

I remember seeing a news feature story several years ago about a young woman and her crippling arachnophobia. Her fear of spiders had become so great that she sought professional counseling. What she didn't bargain for was the radical therapy program she would experience.

The initial sessions gave her an opportunity to talk about her fear and face the reality of how it was negatively impacting her life. The next step was to begin gradually introducing her into an environment with spiders.

First, a small common house spider that was in a glass container was brought into the room with her—far across the room. Initially, she went into a panic. But as she repeatedly faced her fear and sat in the same room as a caged little spider, she began to find freedom.

Then it was time for the next courageous step in her therapy—being in the same room as a caged tarantula. Again, there was initial panic followed by freedom. The freedom wasn't so much not having any anxiety about the presence of the spider but was rather not being controlled by fear.

Her final therapy session involved actually holding a spider in her hand, which she did successfully without a panic attack. She had turned her fear on its head and overcame its control of her life.

Finding freedom from bitterness requires a radical therapy— forgiveness. Taking on the heart of Christ and forgiving our offenders is the only antidote for bitterness. Forgiveness turns bitterness on its head and overcomes its joy-robbing domination in our lives.

RESTORATION

Billy and his dad, friends of our family, are car enthusiasts— particularly classic sports cars. Billy bought his first one several years ago. It was a 1975 MGB Roadster and was showing its age. Cars, like people, deteriorate over time.

Some car guys (and ladies) just can't stand to see a classic that has turned into a pile of rust and is only good for some spare parts. They find great pleasure in restoring an old car to a thing of beauty.

Over the period of a year or so, instead of letting it land in the junkyard, Billy restored that 1975 MGB Roadster and turned it into something beautiful.

God is into restoration too. He is passionate about restoring people who are broken and beaten down. He takes great pleasure in bringing back blessing where all there seemed to be was loss, heartache, confusion, or frustration.

Where there is brokenness, God is always working to bring about wholeness again. The great drama of the ages is the restoration project of God for a world broken by the Fall. This restoration project is the story of the Bible. It is also the story of our lives.

The effect of living in a broken world and of being broken ourselves is frustration, failure, pain, suffering, etc. God specializes in entering into the broken places (whether self-inflicted, the result of others' actions, or something that is simply a mystery) and turning it for our good. This was the experience of Joseph in the Old Testament, who said of all the trouble he had been through because of his brothers, "You intended to harm me, but God intended it for good to accomplish what is now being done, the saving of many lives." (Genesis 50:20)

Restoration is God's work of turning the tables on Satan, the enemy of our soul. Satan seeks to use our broken places against us to destroy us. God works to use our broken places for the benefit of us and others and for His good purposes.

God's restorative work in Job's story was in direct relationship to the particular things Satan had taken from Job. It was a restoration of wealth, health, and family. But the message of Job 42 for us is not about prosperity; it is about restoration. The specifics of Job's restoration are the specifics for Job; they may not necessarily be the specifics for you or for me.

Restoration will look different for each one of us. It will be unique to our own stories and to the specific work that God is doing in our lives. We may want God to write the kind of ending to our stories that He did for Job, but it is important that we don't insist on our own version of "happily ever after." To do so may actually cause us to miss the blessing God is trying to bring to us, because we are expecting it to happen differently than the way in which He is working.

In addition to not insisting that restoration look a certain way, it is important to remember that when God brings restoration it will change us. When Billy restored his Roadster, it ended up a different color than its original one. The black paint that had grown faded, dingy, and scratched was replaced with powder blue. There would have been nothing wrong with painting it black again, but Billy wanted to make it bright and colorful.

Restoration is not merely putting things back the way they were; it takes the good that was ruined and makes it good again, only better this time.

BEAUTY FROM ASHES

Buffy and I, along with our two children, spent a recent Christmas Eve and Christmas day at my sister's home. My parents and one of my brothers and his wife were also there. It was a special time as we simply enjoyed each other's company.

The scene was picture perfect on Christmas Eve. My sister's two daughters, ages 8 and 6 at the time, were in their pajamas anxiously awaiting the reading of the classic *T'was the Night Before Christmas* while we talked and ate. The time had finally come for everyone to gather in the living room where a fire had been started in the fireplace.

First, my father read the Christmas story from the New Testament book of Luke. Then the baton was passed to my brother-in-law who, with one of his girls on each side of him, read *Twas the Night Before Christmas*. Maggie and Zoe soon were off to bed while the adults lingered for a while in front of the crackling fire.

The fire was going again the next day, this time with toys strewn about the living room floor. Some of the family were in the kitchen getting our Christmas dinner ready. Others were in the family room watching television. A few of us were in the living room watching the fire and talking about sports, politics, and other matters of interest.

My son was tending to the fire at one point when I took particular notice to the ash that had been left from the numerous pieces of wood which had been burned from the night before and so far that day. I looked at the size of the piece of firewood Paul was putting on the fire and realized how little of it would be left in just an hour or so. It would be reduced to ash.

I thought about the ash laying there in the bottom of the fireplace. The wood is gone; it has been broken down to its most elemental form. The gray-black material that remains looks to be of no value. It almost seems to be a waste of a good piece of wood.

But fireplace ash is not worthless, and it doesn't have to be a waste. It can be used as a nutrient for a variety of plants in flower and vegetable gardens. Further, it acts as a slug repellent when worked into the soil. Beauty can come forth from the ashes.

When we have been broken down by life's challenges and mysteries, it doesn't have to be a waste. God works the ashes from our pain into the soil of our lives to bring about new seasons of growth and productivity. He brings beauty from the ashes.

So much of Job's life had been left in an ash heap. As agonizing as losing his wealth, the respect of his friends, and his health had been, nothing could have been as painful as losing all ten of his children. The grief would have been inexpressible. To only deepen the agony, he had been told that his children deserved to die.

Job's story didn't end there. He had seven more sons and three more daughters. Once again he had ten children. Even though there still would have been a lingering ache in his heart for the children he had lost, his additional children certainly brought him great joy.

The daughters in particular were a source of delight and blessing.

Nowhere in all the land were there found women as beautiful as Job's daughters, and their father granted them an inheritance along with their brothers. (Job 42:15)

Two significant things stand out in this verse in light of the ancient cultural backdrop.

First, there is the mention of the extraordinary beauty of Job's three additional daughters. A person's stature was determined to a significant measure by the number of children they had. Two things mattered in particular—that you had one or more sons to pass your inheritance to and that you had beautiful daughters. So when Job had ten more children, he didn't just get a family again for which to love and care; he was esteemed within his community. Such beautiful daughters in addition to having sons meant he was highly esteemed and favored.

Second, there is the mention that Job granted the daughters part of the inheritance. This would be virtually unheard of in ancient cultures. The inheritance passed to male children. Job's three girls held a beauty in his eye that was far beyond physical attractiveness or esteem they brought him. He took great delight in the children God had given him, including the girls, who normally in that culture would not have been so valued.

Out of the ashes came a new respect for women. Considering the cultural context in which Job lived, how beautiful is that. The beauty coming from the ashes was a family to love, but it was also more. It was a man who had been transformed through the pain.

For all of us, the real beauty that comes from the ashes is the transformation that struggling in the mystery brings to our lives.

FULLNESS OF LIFE

It was a gut wrenching decision to accept an offer that was made to me to take a leadership position at the district level of our denomination. Don't get me wrong; I was honored to have been approached about the position. It would mean going from providing pastoral leadership of a single congregation to assisting in the oversight of 80 churches. But Buffy and I were having the time of our lives in the church I had been leading for over eight years.

We desired to be where God wanted us, so we waited for Him to make things clear. That clarity didn't come quickly. For three months we struggled in the mystery as we wrestled with whether or not to accept the offer. Some days we thought I should move ahead with it; other days the thought of leaving the church we deeply loved and enjoyed was so unbearable that we just wanted to say "No, thank you." In fact, one evening I had come to the point of determining to call the district office the next morning to withdraw myself from consideration. But when morning came, I was deeply unsettled about making the call.

Eventually God reached out from the mystery and made it clear to us what to do. Two and a half months later Buffy and I stood in the empty house where we had lived since our two children had been in second and third grades. Everything had been moved to our new home, and we were there that Saturday to clean. The next morning would be my final message at the church.

It was around 10:00 pm when everything was finally done with me having just finished vacuuming the living room. Buffy and I stood there in the quiet, empty room for a while as we experienced a full range of emotions. I could picture so many wonderful things (and some not so wonderful) that had happened there.

Trying to put into words some of what was going on inside of me, I said to Buffy, "Wow, our kids grew up here."

"So did we," she said.

Certainly there was a sense of sadness that evening, but there was also an equally powerful sense of fullness. We realized that night, probably more than ever before, how rich and full our lives had become. We understood those memories not simply as individual good times (or bad times) that stood alone, but as pieces of fabric woven together into the tapestry of our lives. Each of those pieces had formed and shaped us into who we were as we stood there that evening realizing that not only had our kids grown up, but that we had too.

Those five months turned our life upside down. But it was in the unsettling, in the undoing of our comfort zones, that we were able to see something beyond the rush of day to day routines and busyness. We were able to see that so much of our story is far more than making it through another day or another week of activity.

Our calendars are full, but are our lives? Erwin McManus writes: "Deeper than our instinct to live is our longing to be alive. Aliveness is different from existence. The latter is a struggle to survive; the former a thirst for life."[9]

Job had been pushed to the brink during his long ordeal. He wondered at points if he could bear another day, even longing for death because existing was so physically, emotionally, and spiritually exhausting. Now at the end of his struggle, we see him experiencing aliveness.

The fullness of Job's life is not derived from the material prosperity that is noted in Job 42; it is found in what is in between the references to that prosperity. It is discovered in the experience of simple joys. "All his brothers and sisters and every-one who had known him before came and ate with him in his house." (Job 42:11)

How many meals had Job eaten with family and friends before his ordeal? How often had he entertained guests? Certainly this time was different. The laughter was sweeter. The aromas of cooking food were more appetizing. The taste of the meal was savored more. Why had something so simple as the fellowship of people and the joy of a meal with them become so pleasant?

Job had been undone. When he finally came to the end of himself, God was there to fill him up with a different quality of living. It shifted from the material to the spiritual, from Job to God.

The book of Job ends summarily describing the rest of Job's life.

> After this, Job lived a hundred and forty years; he saw his
> children and their children to the fourth generation. And so
> he died, old and full of years. (Job 42:16-17)

This ending is not unlike the way so many good stories end with those familiar words "and they lived happily ever after." But how do we properly understand Job's "happily ever after" ending?

When Snow White lived happily ever after, that didn't mean she never experienced problems ever again. She didn't have the queen to worry about, but I would guess there were challenges that came with living with the prince. When Rachel made it off the plane and she and Ross resolved their confusing relationship to be committed to each other, that didn't mean they would never fight ever again.

In the same way, Job didn't spend the next one hundred forty years without any problems or troubles ever again. There would have been so many ups and downs in that span of time, other mysteries that he faced. None would have been like the defining ordeal that is recorded in the book that bears Job's name, but life didn't become constant bliss. Yet it was a full life.

The last three words of Job are "full of years." We often read that expression as a restatement of the previous word—"old." We often understand it as descriptive of the one hundred and forty years. Thus "old and full of years" is thought of as "old and having had many years."

"Full of years" is connected to how many there were; however rather than restating the fact another way, it amplifies the quality of those many years. They were years of fullness. At the end of all Job had been through, he could still experience being fully alive. In addition to bringing restoration and beauty from the mystery, God brought fullness of life too.

For the mystery to serve its purpose in our lives, we must come to the end of ourselves just as Job had. Erwin McManus captures the pathway to fullness of life this way:

> While we strive to fill ourselves and remain empty, Jesus emptied Himself and lived fully. While we exhaust our energies protecting our personal rights and looking out for ourselves, Jesus, in contrast, who was in His very nature God, did not consider equality with God something He had to hold on to. He made Himself nothing. The journey we are invited to take looks nothing like Narcissus and everything like Jesus.[10]

Throughout our lives there are many stories. There are stories of fair weather and failure, dreams and disappointments, love and loss. The mysteries of life have a way of turning our world upside down. It unsettles; it brings uncertainty; it causes pain. But in the end, it is also an opportunity to discover in a new way what it means to be alive.

ACKNOWLEDGEMENTS

Living in the Mystery had its beginning in 2005 when I did a preaching series in the Old Testament book of Job. When I started preparing for that series of messages, I had little idea how much I would be impacted personally by Job's experience or that it would eventually lead to writing a book. I had the opportunity to teach a condensed version of that series of messages two years later at a summer camp. Again, I was impacted deeply, and it was humbling to observe how God used those messages in the lives of others.

Another two years passed before I set forth to develop these two series of messages into a book. The amount of energy of focus that would be required to write this book was unexpected, and I would not have completed the project without the support, encouragement, and help of many people.

First on that list of people who made this book possible is my wife, Buffy. She encouraged me through times of writer's block and graciously shared more than a few of our evening snacks with me while I typed away at the laptop. She read portions of my writing when I wasn't sure if I had communicated well and gave me her gut reaction feedback. Many of the insights and observations shared in this book are drawn from an interesting diversity of experiences she and I have had the privilege to share over the years we have been together. If it weren't for her standing behind me through this project, I likely would not have finished. Thank you so much, Buffy.

I am grateful for my children, Paul and Adrean, and for my parents, Don and Faith Weidman. Aside from my wife, these four special people have always been my biggest cheerleaders in ministry. It was no less so with writing this book. I hope how much my kids and my parents mean to me comes through in the various stories in which they appear throughout this book. They each motivated me forward during this project by periodically asking me a simple question, "How's your book going?"

Special thanks go to Billy Beveridge, a talented young man who is not only a family friend but also a gifted artist. I asked if he could design a cover for me and described to him the concept for the book. When he brought back his first proposal, I knew I had my cover. He had captured visually what was happening in my mind's eye as I thought about the theme of this book.

I am thankful for the special contribution Laurie Cook made to this book becoming a reality. She reviewed my completed manuscript and provided editorial assistance to get the book ready for publishing.

Writer and conference speaker, Dannah Gresh, encouraged me in my writing. Her review and feedback on some of my early work on the project was very helpful. Thank you, Dannah, for having taken an interest in my desire to write this book.

I also want to express my gratitude for two ministry colleagues and friends, Tim Hickman and Jayne Wilcox. In addition to reading and providing feedback on the first few chapters I had written for this book, they encouraged me that this was a worthy project to complete and have been additional cheerleaders of mine.

There are many others whom I've not named that have in some way contributed to my life and ministry and to the completion of this book. Thanks to all of you as well.

NOTES

1 Found at http://science.howstuffworks.com/quicksand.htm, last accessed on March 30, 2010.
2 Found at http://science.howstuffworks.com/quicksand2.htm, last accessed on March 30, 2010.
3 Stanley Grenz and John Franke, *Beyond Foundationalism: Shaping Theology in a Postmodern Context* (Westminster John Knox Press, 2001), p.120.
4 Quoted in Warren W. Wiersbe, *Be Patient* (Victor Books, 1991), p.56.
5 Robert A. Watson, W. Robertson Nicoll (editor), *The Expositor's Bible: The Book of Job* (Hodder & Stoughton), p.244.
6 Quoted in Warren W. Wiersbe, *Be Patient*, p.110.
7 A. W. Tozer, *The Knowledge of the Holy* (Harper & Brothers, 1961), p.9.
8 J. I. Packer, *Knowing God*, 1993 edition (InterVarsity Press, 1973), p.29.
9 Erwin Raphael McManus, *Uprising: A Revolution of the Soul* (Thomas Nelson, 2003), pp.9-10.
10 Ibid., pp.33-34.